A practical guide to navigating grandparenting today

grand parents

MICHAEL CARR-GREGG

ALLEN & UNWIN
SYDNEY • MELBOURNE • AUCKLAND • LONDON

First published in 2023

Allen & Unwin
Cammeraygal Country
83 Alexander Street
Crows Nest NSW 2065
Australia
Phone: (61 2) 8425 0100
Email: info@allenandunwin.com
Web: www.allenandunwin.com

Allen & Unwin acknowledges the Traditional Owners of the Country on which we live and work. We pay our respects to all Aboriginal and Torres Strait Islander Elders, past and present.

NATIONAL LIBRARY OF AUSTRALIA

A catalogue record for this book is available from the National Library of Australia

ISBN 978 1 76106 931 4

Internal design by Mika Tabata
Index by Puddingburn Publishing Services
Set in 12/18 pt Minion Pro by Midland Typesetters, Australia
Printed and bound in Australia by Pegasus Media & Logistics

10 9 8 7 6 5 4 3 2

MIX
Paper from responsible sources
FSC www.fsc.org FSC® C008194

The paper in this book is FSC® certified. FSC® promotes environmentally responsible, socially beneficial and economically viable management of the world's forests.

Dr Michael Carr-Gregg is an adolescent psychologist, a well-respected speaker and one of Australia's leading parenting authorities. In 1985 he founded Canteen, the acclaimed cancer patients' support group for teenagers in New Zealand and Australia.

Michael has been a contributor on Melbourne radio 3AW, the resident parenting expert on Channel 7's *Sunrise* and a regular guest on its *Morning Show*. He has written several bestselling books on parenting, including *Surviving Adolescents*, *The Princess Bitchface Syndrome* and *Surviving Year 12*. Michael has also worked with organisations including ReachOut and Beyond Blue and has been the 'agony uncle' for *Girlfriend* magazine. He has won many awards for his work.

'For over twenty years Dr Michael Carr-Gregg has provided accurate, up-to-date and reliable information laced with humour and compassion to Australia's parents. In this brilliant new book he has managed to do the same for the country's grandparents.'
Melissa Doyle, journalist and bestselling author of *Fifteen Seconds of Brave*

'Grandparenting can be one of the richest experiences life has to offer. It can also be fraught. Michael Carr-Gregg's handy guide offers a commonsense manual alerting us grandparents to possible pitfalls (and there are many!), and suggesting ways of negotiating them. From being grandparents to newborns, through infancy, childhood, adolescence and young adulthood: each stage demands adjustments, but can, with careful attention, hold much joy and satisfaction for grandparents—and for their grandchildren.' **Margaret Throsby, broadcaster**

'Being a grandparent should be one of life's great joys and here Michael Carr-Gregg has a very practical guide on how to savour the delights and sort the challenges.' **Neil Mitchell, journalist and 3AW presenter**

'A fantastic resource for grandparents that carries a wise reminder to always be respectful of both parents and grandchildren!' **Petrea King, bestselling author *Your Life Matters* and CEO of the Quest for Life Foundation**

'An absolute must-read for all aspiring and established grandparents, and also pretty darn useful for parents too! Another gem from a psychologist who knows how to hit exactly the right mark.' **Dr Helen Street, applied social psychologist and wellbeing consultant**

'Written like a conversation with one of your wisest friends, *Grandparents* is a compassionate and in-depth exploration of what it means to be a modern grandparent and how best to support your grandchildren through the diverse challenges they'll face. A must-read for grandparents at any stage of their journey, filled with practical, comprehensive and affirming advice you'll turn to again and again.' **Ashleigh Barton, bestselling author of *What Do You Call Your Grandma?* and *What Do You Call Your Grandpa?***

To my grandmothers, Lily Rona (1893–1958)
and Sarah Jane 'Daisy' Pride (1886–1955)

Contents

Introduction xi

1 The importance of grandparents 1

2 Preparing for a milestone moment 20

3 The birth 35

4 Getting to know your grandchild 50

5 The power of play 71

6 Screentime 89

7 Grandparenting teens 113

8 Dealing with divorce, separation and loss 132

9 LGBTQIA+ grandchildren 144

10 Transgender grandchildren 156

11 Neurodiverse grandchildren 171

12 Preserving your family's history 189

13 Grandparenting superglue 201

14 Saying goodbye 210

15 The Grandparenting Code 218

Afterword 238
Your grandchild record 240
Acknowledgements 244
Notes 246
Resources 256
Index 269

Grandparenting stories

Reading with your grandchild by Jackie French 18

The last great love of our lives by Kevin Rudd 33

The unflinching honesty of grandchildren by David Williamson 47

What your grandchildren (and their parents) teach you by Jane Caro 87

Connecting with an older grandchild by Jenny Kee 110

The peculiar pain of separated grandparents by Hugh Mackay 130

Reflections of a Type A grandfather by Professor Gordon Parker 187

Being a great grandparent by Eric Tweedale 199

Introduction

When I was a psychologist in training, it was drummed into me that parents have the most powerful influence on a child. What was never acknowledged was the fact that grandparents are, hands down, the second-most powerful influence in a child's life. In many cases—with the possible exception these days of TikTok!—a grandparent is the most important influence on their grandchild's life.

Due to improved life expectancy, the proportion of people who are grandparents has increased around the world. It has been estimated that of the world's 8 billion people, a record-breaking 18 per cent, or 1.5 billion, are currently grandparents.[1] Not only are grandparents living longer—up from an average of just over 70 years in 1960 to 82.9 years today—but they are typically more educated and enjoy better health than previous generations. By 2050, *The Economist* predicts, there will be 2.1 billion grandparents, making up a wonderful 22 per cent of humanity.[2]

At the same time, families are shrinking. Over the same period, from 1960 to now, the average number of children in each family has dropped from five to 2.4. Together, this means the ratio of living grandparents to children is steadily increasing. According to the Australian Bureau of Statistics (ABS) report on 'Grandparents who are the primary carers of their grandchildren' from 2018, there were approximately 31,000 Australian grandparents who provided primary care for their grandchildren. By 2021, this figure had doubled to 62,100 grandparents, which represents 3 per cent of all grandparents in Australia.[3] Grandparents are perhaps more important than ever before.

Close inspection of the data reveals that, while most of Australia's grandparents are Baby Boomers (born between 1946 and 1964), they are not all the same. (The Baby Boomers preceded Generation X, who were born between 1965 and 1979. Then came Generation Y, born between 1980 and 1994, followed by Generation Z, born between 1995 and 2010. The Boomers are now also grandparenting Generation Alpha—anyone born in 2011 or later.) Some people become grandparents comparatively young, when they are still in the workforce, while others may be retired or approaching retirement. Trying to form a picture of the 'classic grandparent' is like trying to pick up mercury with a fork.

But what we do know is that there are more grandparents today, and they are going to be around for longer. Indeed, some of the people reading this book could be grandparents for 30 years, which is almost twice as long as the period in which they parented their own children in their home.

Social scientists tell us that grandparents make an amazing contribution, and this is occasionally acknowledged by politicians. For instance, in 2014, the United Kingdom's prime minister, David Cameron, lauded the nearly 6 million 'unsung heroes' who devoted their time to caring for their grandchildren, saying that they saved Britons over £7 billion ($11.7 billion) in annual childcare costs.[4]

It was estimated in 2018 that Australian grandparents clocked up an average of 58 childcare hours per month, worth $3.94 billion annually, helping to ease the burden on household finances by providing days of 'greycare'—essentially, voluntary childcare—every year.[5]

Even before the Covid-19 pandemic, grandparents were the psychological Araldite that held Australian families together, being the biggest providers of informal childcare for children between birth and twelve years, but particularly for babies and toddlers—especially while their parents were working or studying.[6] Their absence was keenly felt during the pandemic, particularly in those parts of Australia that had prolonged lockdowns. Restrictions on visitations made many parents realise how much they and their children valued the connection with grandparents, and that living life through a screen was a most inadequate substitute.

But it wasn't just the accessible childcare that was missing. Australian and international research suggests that children find unparalleled acknowledgement and love in their relationships with grandparents, and that this has quantifiable emotional, educational and other advantages.

So, why write a book on grandparenting? Well, as far as I can see, there aren't any contemporary Australian guides to grandparenting—a situation not dissimilar to that for parenting half a century ago. And the role of grandparents is simply more important now than ever before.

In fact, the teenagers who read my books on dealing with their adolescence—the first of which, *Adolescence* (written with Erin Shale), came out in 2002, followed by *Surviving Adolescents* (2005) and *The Princess Bitchface Syndrome* (2006)—are now having their own children, so the parents who first bought those books will now be becoming grandparents.

Most first-time grandparents admit that they feel unprepared for the role. They are unsure how to approach it, and some are anxious about stepping on the toes of their kids—the new parents. I get the feeling that many Australian grandparents just white-knuckle their way through, learning as they go along. But as with all major life transitions, becoming a grandparent is an invitation to grow, and the secret to success lies in the preparation.

Australia's rising life expectancy means it is now more common for a child to grow up with grandparents, which brings new opportunities and challenges for intergenerational family relationships. In addition, socioeconomic changes mean that there are more mothers in paid work, greater labour market instability, and higher rates of divorce and relationship breakdown, all of which can mean an increasing role for grandparents in family life.

Grandparents are vital to the emotional care of grandchildren from infancy to adolescence, but also as sources of social and economic support as their children attempt to balance work and family responsibilities and deal with the financial difficulties associated with precarious and/or low-paid jobs. At the same time, however, grandparents' involvement in the extended family is being confronted by increasing pressures for them to defer their retirement from the workforce.

Over the years I've had some extraordinarily rich experiences in talking with Australians. For many years I had the privilege of being the 'agony uncle' for one of Australia's top girls' magazines, *Girlfriend*. I was the family psychologist on Channel 7's *Sunrise* for over a decade, and I remain a social commentator on radio 3AW in Melbourne.

In these various capacities I've had the opportunity to talk to thousands of different kinds of families—gay, straight, transgender, single parents, blended families, parents of children with special needs and those who have been through unimaginable grief, loss or trauma. Some of the most amazing stories I heard were from or about grandparents who had, without any formal advice, figured out by themselves the right path to take. They shared incredible insights and wisdom as they became spectators and their own children became parents themselves.

Many wonder whether grandparents should be proactive, setting goals for their grandkids and for their relationship with them, or reactive, intervening only when there's a serious issue or when the parents ask for help. All the grandparents I've met professed a desire to be helpful and significant to their grandkids, to be effective and to make a difference, but they have so many questions. Some of these are listed here:

- What does the research say about the impact of grandparenting?
- What are the top tips for a first-time grandparent?
- How should grandparents respond to the news of pregnancy and birth?
- What are the biggest mistakes grandparents can make?
- How should grandparents deal with grandchildren and screens?
- Can grandparents be custodians of the family's history?
- What's the best way to grandparent long-distance?
- How should grandparents engage with grandchildren whose parents are separated, divorced or dead?
- What's the best way to grandparent teenagers?
- Which grandparenting strategies and ideas are most effective?
- Are there any circumstances in which a grandparent should criticise their child's parenting?
- If there are several grandchildren, should they all be treated the same or should grandparents focus on those with the greatest need?
- How can grandparents get to know their grandchildren individually, independent of their parents?
- Are there any crucial pieces of life advice grandparents ought to pass on to their grandchildren?

I'll seek to answer these questions and more in this book. I have organised my advice into what I have chosen to call the Grandparenting Code. You may not agree with all of its points, but by the time you finish the book you'll be crystal clear on what I believe and why.

This advice has been augmented by the insights of some well-known Australian grandparents: Jane Caro, Jackie French, Jenny Kee, Hugh Mackay, Professor Gordon Parker, Kevin Rudd and David Williamson. My special thanks go to 102-year-old Eric Tweedale, a Wallabies prop forward between 1946 and 1949, who provides a unique historical perspective. They have all generously and enthusiastically shared their knowledge and wisdom about their grandparenting journey. I am particularly grateful for how their stories paint a picture of modern Australian grandparenting.

I spent much of my early life in New Zealand and it is important to note that I learned much from Māori culture, where grandparents hold a significant role and are highly respected. They are often referred to as 'kaumātua' or 'kuia', which means elder or respected elder, and are very involved in the upbringing of their grandchildren. Māori grandparents are regarded as the link between the past and the present, and put a high priority on passing on knowledge and wisdom to younger generations, especially in teaching them about their whakapapa (genealogy), cultural heritage, language and traditions, which helps younger generations understand their family connections and cultural identity.

This book is written for every conceivable type of grandparent: from those who are about to become grandparents, to those who now have teenage grandkids. All phases and styles of being a grandparent carry challenges, and it's my aim to provide you with practical advice on a wide variety of topics, including how to play with a toddler, what to do about screens, managing family politics, power struggles, and tips on grandchildren who are LGBTQIA+ or neurodiverse. All the advice is based both on evidence and on lived experience, about how to be the best grandparent you can be.

Good grandparenting may not stop the war in Ukraine or address global warming, food insecurity, the energy crisis, inflation and the rising cost of living. But young people today are, of course, the future. And the more willing and involved adult carers there are who are helping them become good human beings, the better. Parents get support and more time for themselves, and the young people get the emotionally uncomplicated love of a grandparent. Everyone benefits. From the hugs, the sleepovers, your new name and general silliness, to the extra source of love, this bond is special and unbreakable. It's a relationship based on love, appreciation, fun and pure joy. Becoming a grandparent is one of the key transitions of a person's life, and inside every transition is an invitation to grow and devote yourself to the role.

ONE

The importance of grandparents

I wonder how many of you remember the year 1955? Australia's population was just under 3.5 million people. Robert Menzies was prime minister, you were listening to Bill Haley and the Comets sing 'Rock Around the Clock', and you may have watched Toparoa win the Melbourne Cup.

It was also the year in which two researchers, Professor Emmy Werner and Ruth Smith, working in Hawaii, were making psychological history. They set out to answer a question to which all grandparents would love to know the answer: what makes resilient young people?

And so the island of Kauai became the setting for one of the most important studies in the field of child psychology, the findings of which remain highly relevant to grandparents in the post-Covid era. You may know Kauai as the location of the 1993 movie *Jurassic Park*, in which terrifyingly realistic dinosaurs ran amok, trying to chow down on Sam Neill and Laura Dern.

The Kauai Longitudinal Study tracked 698 children from their birth in 1955 to adulthood. They suffered from varying degrees of disadvantage, such as prenatal stress (the exposure of an expectant mother to psychosocial or physical stress), chronic poverty, parents who had not graduated from high school, or family environments characterised by parental alcoholism or mental illness. A team of mental health workers, paediatricians, public health nurses and social workers checked in with the study participants when they were aged one, two, ten, eighteen, 32 and 40.

You might think that all young people growing up amid such adversity would struggle in adulthood. But the researchers discovered that while two-thirds of the participants did struggle, one-third actually did very well in their lives. Werner and Smith called them 'vulnerable, but invincible'.

What enabled these young people to thrive in spite of their upbringing? Even though these children were surrounded by potentially debilitating 'risk factors', the group that showed the most resilience were those who had access to buffering elements known as 'protective factors'. Werner and Smith found that one of the key protective factors that distinguished the resilient boys and girls from their at-risk peers was that they'd had the opportunity to establish, early on, a close bond with at least one competent, emotionally stable person who was sensitive to their needs: the so-called 'charismatic adult'.

On Kauai, most of this nurturing came from auxiliary caregivers, such as grandparents. Resilient children seemed to be especially adept at 'recruiting' such surrogate parents. Resilient youngsters tended to rely on elders and peers in their community for emotional support, and sought them out for counsel in times of crisis.

The other protective factors Werner and Smith uncovered were that the charismatic adults taught the children social skills (conflict resolution, anger management, problem-solving and decision-making); made sure that they had a spark, an 'island of competence' (sport, art, music, dance, drama); gave them a sense of meaning, purpose and belonging; and modelled optimistic self-talk. More on these later.

The study reinforced the fact that children do best when they have someone consistently in their lives who will make them feel safe, valued and listened to; with whom they have a sense of connection, meaning, purpose and belonging; and who is adept at conflict resolution, anger management and problem-solving. In other words, someone who can provide an anchor to help them weather life's adversities.

A vital job we as grandparents have is to prepare our young people for an uncertain future. Werner and Smith have given us a template we can use, so that our grandkids do not end up like the brachiosaurs and dilophosaurs of *Jurassic Park*.

As Werner and Smith's study demonstrates, we can help young people build their resilience by being the charismatic adult in their lives, even someone who can act as a mediator between parents and grandchildren. Not only does the presence of a grandparent help the young person feel safe, valued and listened to, but research suggests that grandparents also help their grandchildren grow up to be kinder, more empathetic adults.[1]

So grandparents are in a tremendous position to teach their grandchildren social and emotional competencies, such as how to manage their anger, how to resolve conflicts and solve problems, and how to make good decisions. These are the lessons that ultimately make for an easier passage through life.

WHAT ARE THE MAIN COMPONENTS OF RESILIENCE?

The American Psychological Association outlines four core components of resilience: connection, wellness, healthy thinking, and meaning.[2] They argue that a focus on these four components can enable your grandchild to withstand and learn from difficult and traumatic experiences.

- *Connection*: Encourage your grandchild to prioritise healthy relationships with empathetic and understanding peers, so that they are reminded they are not alone during difficulties. Having access to trustworthy and compassionate people who validate their feelings will support the skill of resilience.
- *Wellness*: Help them take care of their body by practising proper self-care, including good nutrition, exercise, sleep, hydration and mindfulness.
- *Healthy thinking*: Encourage them to maintain healthy thought patterns, such as keeping things in perspective, accepting that change is inevitable and striving to maintain a positive attitude.

- *Meaning*: Help them find their purpose and a sense of belonging. Encourage them to help others, to be a proactive problem-solver during hard times, and to set and work towards realistic goals. Encourage them to feel part of something bigger than themselves—to foster a sense of connectedness and relatedness that transcends the material world.

Myths about grandparents

We need to acknowledge from the outset that none of us are flawless. There is no such thing as the perfect parent or grandparent. Many of the grandparents I interviewed for this book were remarkably candid about the mistakes they had made. Having grandchildren can be an emotional rollercoaster, and sometimes our judgement can be flawed.

In order to become the charismatic adult in the life of your grandchild, you have to start early. Society has no shortage of ideas about what it means to be a good grandparent, but how do we steer through the myths and avoid useless stereotypes?

If you're like me and your grandparents died before you were born, or if you were too young to remember them, then much of your education about how to be a grandparent may have come from less-than-helpful depictions on television and in film. Think of Grandpa Joe from *Willie Wonka & the Chocolate Factory*, Endora from *Bewitched*, Abe Simpson from *The Simpsons*, the Dowager Countess Violet Crawley from *Downton Abbey* and Jay Pritchett from *Modern Family*.

So let's dispense with the stereotypes and instead look at some evidence-based research.

MYTH 1—Grandparents are old, frail and sedentary

While many grandparents may be older and some may have health issues, not all grandparents fit this stereotype. Many are active and healthy and enjoy participating in a wide range of activities.

The old and frail stereotype is reinforced by television shows and movies that depict grandmothers as diminutive, slightly decrepit, grey-haired ladies sitting in rocking chairs, smelling of lavender and knitting booties. Grandfathers are often shown as myopic, stooped old men with walking frames, pottering around gardens, snoozing or reading newspapers.

The truth is that today's grandparents are far more likely to be active, volunteering at the local op shop, cruising the Great Lakes or going to Kiss concerts. Many of today's grandparents are still working—some are bankers, politicians, pilots or police. Some travel the outback in Winnebagos, throw themselves out of planes at 4000 metres or tour the world in rock bands. (Mick Jagger, for example, has five grandchildren and three great-grandchildren.) One in four males aged 68 is employed full-time, as is one in ten females aged 68.

As Australians are living longer and working longer, these grandparents are active, busy and may have less time to invest in their grandchildren than the stereotype might suggest. This is not to say that younger grandparents aren't enthusiastic about their grandkids, but the reality is that some may have work or social commitments that consume much of their time.

MYTH 2—Grandparents are out of touch with modern technology and culture

While some grandparents may be less familiar with technology and pop culture, many are tech-savvy and keep up with current events and trends. A 2022 survey revealed that almost half of grandparents play video games at least once per month—more than non-grandparents. Daily play is also more common. And contrary to what many might think, it is grandmothers (61 per cent) who hit the Xbox or play on their phones most. Although some gaming grandparents say they play to 'spend time with family', they play solo 80 per cent of the time. Unsurprisingly, grandchildren are their primary source of gaming news, followed by adult friends and family.[3] (For more on screens and how grandparents can manage them, see Chapter 6.)

MYTH 3—Being a grandparent has a rejuvenating effect and results in significant mental and physical health advantages

For many years, there was an assumption that there were measurable mental and physical health advantages for those who provided care for their grandchildren.[4] One 2016 study found that over-65s who took care of grandchildren felt at least two years younger than their age, and this rose to 2.6 years for men aged 74–85.[5] But a 2021 study of data from the German Ageing Survey, published in the *Journals of Gerontology*, revealed that caring for grandchildren failed to make grandparents feel any younger than their actual age.[6] It turned out that the original study only looked at healthy grandparents, so the link likely had more to do with hidden selection effects. But whether or not childcare makes grandparents feel younger, the physical and mental benefits of close family relationships can't be overstated.

MYTH 4—Grandparents are always doting and indulgent

Wrong. While many grandparents are loving and supportive, not all are able to provide the same level of support and attention to their grandchildren. Researchers have identified five different grandparenting styles. 'Traditional Grandparents' are characterised by having a strong sense of tradition and family values, as well as providing guidance, discipline and support for their grandchildren. 'Fun Grandparents' prioritise entertainment, taking grandchildren on outings, holidays and other activities. 'Indulgent Grandparents' are the ones who spoil their grandchildren with gifts and special treats, and they tend to be more lenient about discipline and rules. 'Hands-Off Grandparents' are characterised by a more distant relationship with their grandchildren; this is often found in those who live far away from or have limited contact with their grandchildren. Lastly, 'Mentoring Grandparents' take an active interest in their grandchildren's education and career development, and are keen to offer guidance, support and advice on a variety of topics, such as schoolwork or career choices. Of course, some grandparents may be a blend of these five styles.

MYTH 5—Grandparents don't raise their grandchildren

According to data from the US Census Bureau, in 2019 there were 2.7 million grandparents in the United States who were responsible for the basic needs of one or more grandchildren under the age of eighteen. This number has been steadily increasing over the past few decades, likely due to factors such as the opioid epidemic and other societal changes. In Australia, according to data from the ABS, in 2016 there were approximately 28,900 grandparents who were the primary caregivers for their grandchildren. This represents a very small proportion of Australia's 5 million grandparents, but it's important to note that this number only reflects grandparents who are the primary caregivers, and does not include those who provide occasional or secondary care to their grandchildren. Additionally, the number of grandparents raising their grandchildren may have increased in the years since this data was collected.

MYTH 6—There are no financial support options available in Australia for grandparents who regularly care for their grandchildren

False. One of the main forms of government support is the Grandparent Child Care Benefit, which is a means-tested payment that helps grandparents with the costs of raising their grandchildren. The benefit is available to grandparents who have primary care of their grandchildren for at least 28 per cent of the time, and who meet certain income and residency requirements. The payment amount varies depending on the grandparent's income and the number of children in their care. In addition, grandparents who are providing care for their grandchildren may be eligible for other forms of financial assistance, such as the Family Tax Benefit or the Child Care Subsidy. It's important to note that eligibility and payment amounts may vary depending on individual circumstances.

In some cases, grandparents can become sole primary caregivers. This can happen for a variety of reasons, for example if the grandchildren's parents are unable to care for them due to issues such as addiction, incarceration or illness, or if the grandparents simply choose to take on a larger role in their grandchildren's lives. Occasionally, grandparents may become the legal guardians of their grandchildren, or formally adopt them.

ASSUMPTIONS ABOUT THE ELDERLY

There are other common but misguided assumptions that people make about the elderly, including:

1. That depression and loneliness are normal in older adults. Studies show that older adults are less likely to experience depression than young adults.[7]
2. That they are forgetful. Age-related changes in memory are a normal part of ageing, and older adults may take longer to learn new information and recall it from memory.[8] However, older adults can compensate for these changes by relying on strategies such as repetition, organisation and elaboration.
3. That they are no longer productive. While it's true that some older adults may have retired from their careers or may have reduced physical abilities due to age-related health conditions, many older adults remain active and engaged in various activities that contribute to society.[9] In fact, many older adults continue to work or volunteer in their communities, providing valuable skills, knowledge and experience.

4. That they are all the same. Not all older adults have the same interests, needs and abilities. Just like the members of any other age group, older adults are a diverse group of individuals with unique experiences, interests and needs.

The grandmother effect

In many societies, grandmothers are important 'allomothers'—that is, people who are not an infant's biological mother but who provide care and nurturing—and having access to an invested, engaged, loving grandmother is often associated with improved grandchild health and wellbeing. The earliest recognition of this 'grandmother effect' was documented among the Hadza hunter-gatherers from Tanzania, where grandmothers provision their grandchildren with difficult-to-extract tubers, and this improves grandchild growth.[10]

In virtually every society that has been studied, it turns out that grandmothers provide gargantuan amounts of direct care, such as holding, carrying, cleaning, feeding and supervising infants and children. But the social scientists have found that the benefits go way beyond this practical support. In rural Pakistan, for example, researchers discovered high grandmaternal involvement in direct caregiving is positively associated with cognitive, fine-motor and socioemotional development.[11]

More generally, grandmaternal investment has been associated with improved cognitive functioning, improved academic achievement, and decreased emotional and behavioural problems among children.[12] In a review of alloparental effects in traditional human societies, the presence of a maternal grandmother improved child survival in nine of thirteen societies.[13]

Functional neuroimaging provides a window into the neurobiology of grandmaternal caregiving. Researchers have found that when grandmothers view photos of their grandchild, this activates their brain regions involved in emotional empathy.[14] Furthermore, in comparison with fathers, grandmothers more strongly activate the brain regions involved with emotional empathy, as well as those involved with reward and motivation. While it would be premature to conclude from this study alone that grandmothers are more empathic than fathers, as such studies have their limitations, it certainly suggests that the 'magic' that happens between grandmothers and grandchildren may come from deep within our brains.

THE GRANDMOTHER EFFECT IN TANZANIA

'The Grandmother Effect' is a term used to describe the evolutionary phenomenon in which postmenopausal women (grandmothers) in some species contribute to the survival and reproductive success of their offspring and grandchildren, leading to better nutrition and reproductive success in their families. The concept was first proposed by evolutionary anthropologist Kristen Hawkes and her colleagues in the late 1990s, based on their studies of the Hadza people of Tanzania, an indigenous group that still practises hunting and gathering.[15]

Hawkes and her colleagues found that postmenopausal women in the Hadza community played an important role in helping to care for their grandchildren and in contributing to the food resources of their family group. This support allowed their own offspring to have more children, and as a result the family group's overall reproductive success was increased.

The Grandmother Effect is now recognised as a significant factor in the evolution of human societies and has been observed in other social animals as well, including elephants, orcas and some species of monkeys. The concept highlights the importance of intergenerational cooperation and the unique contributions that older members of a community can make to the survival and success of their families and communities.

A family role model

It is clear from the literature that grandparents can play an important role in the family by providing love, support and guidance to their grandchildren. They can also help to ease the burden on parents by providing additional help for the family.

Grandparents often serve as role models and offer a different perspective on life. They can also provide a sense of continuity and history for the family. Grandparents can provide childcare and help out with tasks such as cooking and transportation. Overall, they can play a vital role in the development and well-being of their grandchildren and of the family as a whole.

In the next chapter, we will consider what it's like when you discover you are going to become a grandparent, and how to best manage the ensuing emotions.

Reading with your grandchild

Jackie French AM

Author, ecologist and historian

You don't actually admit to anyone you have been collecting books for your first grandchild for a decade. But they are there on the shelf, nonetheless, the prize winners bought at every Children's Book Council of Australia conference, signed by the authors; little-known gems discovered in bookshops; others suggested by friends. When you're part of the community of children's literature, you end up with glorious books indeed.

This Christmas, for the first time, I sat with my eighteen-month-old grandchild on my lap, and read to them. Or tried to.

They wriggled, jiggled, giggled and squirmed. Book after book, in all styles and colours—they'd have none of them. Instead, pointing out the window, 'Bird!' they said.

Which might be why, when I carried them past the bookshelf, they pointed to *The Complete Guide to Birds of Australia*. 'Bird!' they demanded.

So we read it, not just the photos but the text too. 'Nest?' they asked. 'Worms? Baby birds? Bird outside!' they announced, as we came to the page with the eastern spinebill they'd seen half an hour before.

We read it for half an hour that time, and many times after that, moving on to *Mammals of Australia*, where they were interested only in the different species of wallabies and kangaroos. But kids' books? According to my grandchild, they are strictly for the birds.

Which is hard, when you're a grandma and an author of children's books. But my grandchild isn't alone. When we surveyed the books Canberra kids were taking out of public libraries, we found that the selections of adolescents were the same as adults', apart from a few favourite authors they stayed loyal to, when any new book appeared. When I ask kids about the books they find fascinating, about one in four likes nonfiction—and it is mainly nonfiction written for adults.

Why not? The 'adult' books are often larger, with more information to absorb, and produced on a larger budget. Kids—even toddlers, like my grandchild—are capable of understanding the text that accompanies any of the natural history 'guides'. We don't tell kids, 'No, you can't watch that adult movie because you won't understand it.' We know they will understand it; the caution is that the themes are too challenging for them emotionally, not intellectually.

If we are to entice kids to be readers, we need to accept that they have a right to choose the books they love.

Even if they aren't Grandma's.

TWO

Preparing for a milestone moment

Most of us (of a certain age) clearly remember the day when Neil Armstrong walked on the moon in 1969, when Diana married Charles in 1981 and when Cathy Freeman won the gold medal in 2000. For many first-time grandparents, another milestone moment that will become etched in your memory is when your child drops the 'B' bomb and reveals that there is a bundle of joy on the way.

This moment is often underplayed, but discovering that there will be a third generation of your family is a significant life event, one that deserves acknowledgement.

People feel a range of emotions when they first learn they are going to become grandparents. Some might be thrilled, ecstatic and proud to be starting a new chapter in their lives. I call this 'foetal attraction'. They might look forward to the opportunity of sharing their wisdom, love and experiences with their grandchild. Others might feel a sense of nostalgia and longing for their own children, who are now grown and starting families of their own. They might also feel some uncertainty or nervousness about their new role as grandparents, and about the new responsibilities that come with it.

This is why I have come up with the Grandparenting Code, a set of guidelines that I hope will be helpful to people starting out on this journey. The full Code is set out in this book's final chapter.

Question time

When you heard the news that your son or daughter was expecting a baby of their own, many questions probably popped into your head: *When did you find out? When is it due? Who have you told?* In my experience, however, this is a moment when some people make the first major mistake of grandparenting.

Your response to this news sets the emotional tone for the immediate future—for your interactions with your child before and after your grandchild's birth. For just as you will always remember hearing this news, it is likely that your child will always recall your response—especially if it is a negative one.

Questions to avoid

It's important to be sensitive and respectful when discussing a loved one's pregnancy, as certain questions can be invasive or uncomfortable. Unwanted responses would include:

- 'Isn't your apartment a bit small?'
- 'I thought you were saving for a house?'
- 'Was the pregnancy planned?'
- 'Are you going to keep the baby?'
- 'Have you thought this through?'
- 'What will happen when you've only got one income?'
- 'I hope you don't expect me to look after it . . .'
- 'Can I be in the delivery room?'
- 'Do you really think you should be bringing a child into this world at this time?'

Although it is normal for your emotions to swing from excitement to trepidation, this is not the time to launch into a lecture. Even if you fundamentally believe that your child's partner is unworthy of your child's love—whether it's because you've diagnosed them with a complex personality disorder or because you think they have the ethics of a cash register—you should muzzle those misgivings for now.

As a future grandparent wishing to start off on the right foot, it is most helpful if your initial response is one of unbridled joy and wonder, and if you can express the support you can offer, whether it be practical, financial or both. There are exceptions to this rule, but it is imperative that you show unconditional love and let your child and their partner know that you are thrilled to bits and will be there for them during and after the pregnancy. What your child needs at this moment is buckets of reassurance that you have their back.

Can you keep a secret?

Sometimes, after dropping the B bomb, your child and their partner may request that you keep the news of the impending child a closely guarded secret. The next part of the Code is to honour the wishes of the couple or person having the baby. Resist the urge to tweet this out to the world. That might be difficult, but not doing so is a serious violation of the Grandparenting Code.

Some parents-to-be, particularly if they have previously had a miscarriage or a sudden infant death, may wish to wait until well after the first scan before spreading the news. Others might just want to protect their privacy and avoid the unwanted attention a pregnancy brings.

Once you do get the green light to share the news, keep in mind that telling your friends that you're expecting your first grandchild might not necessarily elicit the response you expect. But good mates should be genuinely thrilled for you. Some acquaintances may be jealous of your happiness, others may worry about losing your friendship or having less time with you, still others may have unresolved issues with their own children and feel a bit triggered by your news. Whatever the reason, it is important to remember that their reaction is more about them than you. You have the right to celebrate your joy, so invest your time and energy in sharing the news with others who are happy for you.

What to say and not to say

Knowing what to say and when to say it is an important part of grandparenting with grace, and the first few months of a pregnancy will likely test this. This also applies to the delivery of the child. Many grandparents I interviewed had very strong feelings about how and where the baby should be delivered: inductions, home births, water births, elective caesarean and a variety of other options might all come into play at this time.

Unless you are a midwife, obstetrician or other medical practitioner (and perhaps even then!), and until your opinion is sought by the expecting parent(s), it is generally best if you keep your opinion to yourself.

Pregnancy care, prenatal exercises and birth practices are very different today from what they were 30 years ago—ask any birth partner! Prenatal screening and toxoplasmosis were not commonly discussed back then, for instance. The chances are that if you think you know better, you probably don't.

Much like when you discovered you were going to be a grandparent, gestation is a time when your every communication should be about supporting your child and their partner in the decisions that they make. The analogy that comes to mind as I write these words is that grandparents are in the back row of the Shane Warne Stand at the MCG, while your child and their partner are on the field playing the game. You are a spectator cheering them on, so please stay in the psychological bleachers!

The great reassurer

Many couples feel doubt and indecision as they go through pregnancy classes, and the next part of the Code suggests that a grandparent's job is to reassure both parties what great parents they are going to be.

Pregnancy can cause constipation, backache, an increased need to urinate, indigestion, leg cramps, varicose veins, haemorrhoids and nosebleeds—which is why the Code advises not sharing with the expectant person or couple any 'war stories' of how their cousin Imogen's waters broke while she was driving across the Sydney Harbour Bridge, or how Aunt Emma gave birth while flying over the Nullarbor Plain. This sort of advice is unhelpful, so just don't. One client told me that her mother (who had had four difficult deliveries) spent almost an hour telling her daughter how narrow her hips were and what agony she had endured.

George Bernard Shaw once said that the greatest problem in communication is the illusion that it has been accomplished. This is a time for empathy, and for clear, unambiguous messages on high rotation. The key messages that need to be on the grandparenting playlist include:

- 'Congratulations! This is such wonderful news!'
- 'We are so happy for you and can't wait to meet our new grandchild.'
- 'How are you feeling? Is there anything we can do to support you during your pregnancy?'
- 'You're going to be new parents, but we are going to be new grandparents and all of us will be learning on the job—so expect the odd glitch.'
- 'We are keen to help as much as we can.'
- 'If we get it wrong, tell us.'
- 'Have you thought about your plans for prenatal care and delivery? Let us know if you need any help finding resources or making arrangements.'
- 'We are here for you, and we want to help in any way we can, whether that's by babysitting, helping with household chores, or just being there to listen and offer support.'

Let the expectant person or couple know that you are available, but don't phone on a daily basis and interrogate them about whether they are getting enough rest, the contents of their diet and so on. Offering to help with housework, shopping or a back rub, or accompanying them to tests and scans, is much more likely to be appreciated and fondly remembered.

One way to demonstrate your support for the expectant couple is to discover which parenting books, if any, they are reading, and devour them yourself. It doesn't matter if you think that the theories are a mixture of hogwash and bunkum—at least you'll understand why they have chosen to do what it is that they are doing. Be warned, though: there are some pretty interesting theories out there, including the idea that you need to ask baby for their consent before you change their nappy.[1]

The time leading up to the birth can be quite frustrating. Most grandparents tell me that they felt overwhelmed with the desire to help, but some admitted to feeling useless and apprehensive simultaneously. How prepared you are at this time will depend upon your experience with your own grandparents, as well as on the rapport you have with the child who is about to become a parent.[2] Calm, rational discussions before the birth can offset any potential conflicts later on.

A new name for a new role

While many conversations take place at this time, the Code suggests that this could be a good time to discuss how you'd like to be referred to. In some families, the terminology is culturally determined—*nonna* (Italian), *yaya* (Greek), *oma*

(German), *nai nai* (Mandarin)—but in Anglo-Saxon families there are many variations: *grandma*, *nan*, *nanna*, *nanny*, *gran*, *granny* and so on. (Within each culture, of course, there may be regional variations or dialectical differences in the terms used to refer to a grandmother or grandfather.) See the non-exhaustive list of names from different cultures on pages 30–31.

If you adored your maternal grandmother and called her *grandma*, you might like to be called this yourself. Others might have had a more distant relationship and may prefer the more formal *grandmother*. If you have a preference, let your child and their partner know. Now is the time to talk about this issue, especially if it is important to you.

Things to do while waiting

As you are waiting the 273 days for your grandchild to develop in utero, you may be hit by the odd wave of nostalgia. Some grandparents told me that they found it emotionally helpful to create a scrapbook about their experiences and early years, so that they could pass this on to their grandchildren in the future. (For more on this, see Chapter 12.)

It might sound strange, but I have met grandparents who found it immensely satisfying to write a letter to their soon-to-be

WHAT'S IN A NAME?	
GRANDMOTHER	**GRANDFATHER**
English—*Grandma, Granny, Nana, Gran, Grams, Nan*	English—*Grandpa, Gramps, Granddad, Pop, Pappy, Pa*
Aboriginal and Torres Strait Islander[3]—*Gunhinarrung/Badhiin* (Wiradjuri), *Dembart* (Noongar), *Aka* (Torres Strait Creole), *Nanna*	Aboriginal and Torres Strait Islander—*Ngabun/Nabiinbaal* (Wiradjuri), *Demban* (Noongar), *Athe* (Torres Strait Creole), *Pop*
Māori—*Kuia, Tipuna*[4]	Māori—*Koro, Koroua*
Greek—*Yaya*	Greek—*Pappou*
Hindi—*Nani, Dadi*	Hindi—*Nana, Dada*
Mandarin—*Nai Nai, Wai Po*	Mandarin—*Ye Ye, Wai Gong*
Cantonese—*Ngoi Po, Maa Maa*	Cantonese—*Ngoi Gung, Je Je*
Vietnamese—*Ba, Ba cu*	Vietnamese—*Ong, Ong cu*

GRANDMOTHER	GRANDFATHER
Philippines—*Lola, Nanay, Itay*	Philippines—*Lolo, Tatay, Inay*
Nepalese—*Dadi, Aama, Haima, Nani*	Nepalese—*Dada, Buwa, Haju, Baje*
Spanish—*Abuela, Abuelita*	Spanish—*Abuelo, Abuelito*
French—*Grand-mère, Mamie*	French—*Grand-père, Papi*
Italian—*Nonna*	Italian—*Nonno*
German—*Großmutter, Oma*	German—*Großvater, Opa*
Japanese—*Obaasan, Sobo*	Japanese—*Ojiisan, Sofu*
Korean—*Halmoni*	Korean—*Haraboji*
Russian—*Babushka*	Russian—*Dedushka*
Arabic—*Jidda*	Arabic—*Jadd*
Swahili—*Bibi*	Swahili—*Babu*
Turkish—*Anneanne*	Turkish—*Dede*
Polish—*Babcia*	Polish—*Dziadek*
Sudanese—*Jadda, Ayah, Nana*	Sudanese—*Jaddi, Awom Yeye*

grandchild, articulating the excitement, joy and anticipation they were feeling and detailing the plans being made. The letter might describe what the grandchild's parents and siblings are doing, what the nursery looks like, and how much the grandparent is looking forward to the child's arrival and to watching them grow and develop unique talents and interests. Prior to a birth, the letters can be given to the parents to put in a baby book, which may become a treasured part of the family history.

Other grandparents while away these months buying things for the child. This can be a problem, unless, as the Grandparenting Code suggests, the grandparents first have a chat with the expectant parents about what they need and want. Making a quilt, knitting booties, helping out with maternity clothes or buying a cot or stroller can make a big difference to financially stressed parents, and can be a cherished gift.

This pre-birth period is crucial. The Grandparenting Code advises that you don't suffocate or criticise your child and their partner, but focus instead on building bridges; demonstrating compassion, understanding and love; avoiding competition; and offering as much support as you can—and responding when invited.

In the next chapter, we will discuss how you can be of assistance around the time of the birth and beyond. This is where the fun really starts.

The last great love of our lives

Kevin Rudd AC

26th Prime Minister of Australia

My wife Thérèse and I have three grandchildren. Two girls and one boy, ranging in age from ten years to twelve months. They are each a genuine delight, always lighting up the room, even on their naughty days. Thérèse describes them as the last great love of our lives, after our own parents, our own children and, of course, each other.

As with parenting, there are few instruction manuals on how to be a good grandparent. You learn much on the job. I never really knew my own grandparents: one died before I was born; a second when I was barely school-aged; while the others, who lived a world away in rural New South Wales, passed away before I left primary school.

For us, the single most important principle with our own grandchildren has been unqualified love. We simply can't know what little ones go through each day in their lives, particularly once they start school. But it is important that they know they will always receive open arms for a cuddle, a smiling face to greet them and a willing ear to listen. If there is a second principle, it is this: always make time for little ones and play with them within the grain of their interests rather than your own. Their parents are likely to be busy providing for the family and therefore pressed for time. Having the time to simply sit, make some Milo, go fishing or play yet another board game is a precious gift. When ours can't decide what they want to play next, I threaten to read them some of my favourite parliamentary speeches. That's when they run shrieking with laughter from the room, before soon coming back with their own ideas about what they would like to do together instead. They are not little for long, but these are the years when grandchildren and grandparents can become friends for life.

Finally, there is the problem of distance. Then again, there is the solution called FaceTime. However, each conversation should not be a stilted one, starting with, 'How are you?' It should be about where you got up to with the games you were last playing with them, the stories you have heard, the funny photos you send of the pets they love—or, most importantly, the dad jokes you have devised together.

When they were tiny, I have played finger puppets with them from the airport lounge with my own special performances and voices, often to the consternation—but usually the amusement—of my fellow travellers.

Grandkids above all will remember your sense of fun—or lack thereof! We're not perfect at it. But it's not that hard. So good luck.

THREE

The birth

Let's begin this chapter with a discussion of whether grandparents should be present at the birth. Giving birth to a child is an intimate, intensely private experience, so the decision as to who may be present should absolutely depend on the preferences and circumstances of the mother. Today, some 38 per cent of mothers in Australia give birth by caesarean section, which is a major operation, and many hospitals have strict rules that only one relative may be present.[1]

Some of my clients tell me that they could not imagine giving birth without their mother being present, while others offer up a resounding 'no'. Several studies have shown that mother-to-mother support during childbirth can help reduce stress, anxiety and pain for the labouring mother, and can also lead to better birth outcomes such as shorter labour and fewer medical interventions.[2] Whether a grandmother is invited to be present at the birth of her grandchild is likely to depend on the dynamics of her relationship with her daughter. If it's a 'complicated' relationship, with a whole swag of unresolved issues, the daughter may choose someone else, as they may feel (correctly) that it is unlikely that deep-seated, longstanding relationship issues will be resolved simply by having their mother (or anyone else whom they have enmity with) in the birthing suite.

While not all babies arrive on time—some are early, some late—and while most pregnancies progress without incident, about 8 per cent involve complications that, if left untreated, could harm the mother or the baby.[3] But let's assume that, one way or another, your grandchild has arrived. Your support at this time will never be measured by the number of gifts you gave or the frequency of your visits. What matters now, and what will most likely be long remembered, is what you say.

Stay put, unless invited

You'll likely be bursting to see and hold your new grandchild. But the next part of the Code advises caution. Sometimes, less is more. Don't turn up unless you have been invited. This is a bonding time for the new family, so you must be patient. Grandparents should slow down and take a deep breath before making any move.

The day of the birth of your grandchild represents another opportunity not to violate the Code. Irrespective of what has taken place before, grandparents need to revisit the 'unbridled joy' script. Resist the temptation to state any desire for a particular gender, and do not express anything other than immense pride when your son or daughter and their partner share with you the name they have chosen for their child.

Rules for the first visit

When you are invited to meet your grandchild for the first time, an important principle of the Code stipulates—notwithstanding the fact that most newborns look like Winston Churchill—that there is only one correct response: 'What a beautiful baby!' Above all, resist the temptation to stamp the child with your DNA with comments like, 'Look at those ears—just like mine!'

While for some first-time grandparents it can be an overwhelming experience to see, hold and smell this tiny human being for the first time, others become anxious when confronted with the newborn. But relax—not all grandparents immediately bond with their grandchildren. The infatuation can take time to develop, so don't fret if you are not instantly besotted.

Baby names

These days, baby names can be a particular bone of contention.[4] While Charlotte, Amelia, Isla, Oliver and Noah were the most popular baby names in Australia in 2023,[5] if the parents decide to depart from the norm and call their child Jacuzzi, Psamantha (yes, with a P!), Sharlet or Rein Beaux, your job is to say one or all of the following:

- 'Perfect!'
- 'How original!'
- 'How creative!'

After you have swallowed your disappointment that the child wasn't named after you or that some cherished family name has been omitted, remind yourself that this is the couple's decision—not yours.

THE MOST POPULAR BABY NAMES IN AUSTRALIA IN 2023	
GIRLS	**BOYS**
Charlotte	Oliver
Amelia	Noah
Isla	Leo
Olivia	William
Mia	Henry
Ava	Jack
Matilda	Theodore
Ella	Hudson
Grace	Charlie
Willow	Luca

If your grandchild has joined the list of stupid baby names (SBNs) that are so in vogue with tech moguls, singers and A-listers, perhaps you can take comfort that their name wasn't X Æ A-12,[6] Apple, Dream, Bluebell, Rocket Zot or Lyra Antarctica—unless it was, in which case I may be seeing that child in the future. I have heard about a few instances when grandparents were asked for their ideas about baby names, so it's a good idea to have a few of your preferences ready just in case. But don't throw a tantrum if the parents don't like them.

Cocooning

Some grandparents may be surprised by a relatively new trend known as cocooning. This describes an intensive period of care during which parents bring their baby home and elect to live in isolation for weeks, so that the only people to hold, change, feed, touch, kiss, comfort and play with the child are the parents. The aim is to offer a tranquil environment for the newborn, which is supposed to help the child adjust to the new setting, as well as allowing the parents time to gain a sense of control.

The house essentially becomes a 'cocoon' for the parents, who also are trying to protect their child from certain diseases, such as pertussis (whooping cough), until the baby is old enough to be vaccinated. Under the most extreme version of cocooning, the child doesn't leave the house, and new family members—including grandparents—will not be introduced for a set period of time, although digital communication can occur.

Cocooning is not a universal or even a recommended approach to childrearing, and it is, of course, up to individual parents to decide whether it's appropriate for their family. While cocooning can help protect a newborn from infections, it's also important for babies to experience socialisation and stimulation as they grow and develop.

While grandparents must respect the wishes of the parents, parents need to weigh up the benefits against the costs of being secluded, because isolation can be like an echo chamber for difficult thoughts and make the first few weeks of parenthood even more challenging.

If there were any medical complications following the birth, the new parents may require additional help. But any help you give must be delivered in a way that supports them, rather than asphyxiates them. Even in the most tricky of medical circumstances, the baby and their parents will need some time alone. Your desire for a quick cuddle must be put on the backburner.

The first few days

The first few days of your grandchild's life should ideally be spent with their parents. If and when everyone feels up to it, there may be the chance to introduce the child to significant family members and even friends.

COMMON COMPLICATIONS AFTER BIRTH

There are a number of common complications that mothers can experience after birth. These include:

- *Postpartum bleeding*: This is the most common complication and occurs when the uterus does not contract properly after birth, leading to excessive bleeding.
- *Perineal tearing*: During delivery, the area between the vagina and anus (perineum) may tear or be cut to facilitate the delivery of the baby. These tears may require stitches and are painful.
- *Postpartum depression (PPD)*: This is a type of depression that affects some women after childbirth. Symptoms may include sadness, anxiety, irritability and difficulty bonding with the baby.
- *Mastitis*: This is an infection of the breast tissue that can occur when bacteria enter the breast through a cracked or sore nipple.

- *Urinary problems*: Some women may experience difficulty urinating or have bladder-control issues after giving birth.
- *Blood clots*: Women who have recently given birth are at increased risk of developing blood clots in the legs or lungs.
- *Anaemia*: Some women may experience a drop in their red-blood-cell count after delivery, leading to anaemia and fatigue.

It's important for new mothers to be aware of these potential complications and to seek medical attention if they experience any concerning symptoms after giving birth. With proper medical care and support, most complications can be effectively managed or treated.

For first-time parents, this is both a stressful and a joyful time, but it can also be a time when they feel like sitting ducks, exposed to any random relative with good intentions and a casserole under their arm. The roll call of potential well-wishers eager to grab a glimpse of bubs can be a long one, but now is the time for grandparents to model patience, and potentially to do a bit of privacy policing themselves. Don't let people play the geography card—just because they usually live on the other side of the world, they don't have an 'access all areas' pass to this party!

It's always good to ask what the parents would like help with, rather than assume that you know best. You don't want them to feel like you're imposing on them. When you help parents how *they* need it and not how *you* need it, they will be much more inclined to invite you over more often.

In some instances, there are multiple sets of grandparents on hand, and if you are inclined to be involved, remember that grandparenting is not a competitive sport—even if others see it that way. Clear communication and cooperation between all parties can ensure no one feels excluded and create a bond between all generations. Obviously, this is not always achieved; I'm often reminded of something the writer Mary Karr said: 'A dysfunctional family is any family with more than one person in it.'[7]

What happens in the next few months is anyone's guess. Each baby has their own developmental trajectory. One baby might feed long and sleep soundly, while another wants to be fed little and often. One might have dreadful colic and another will be fine.

Sleep deprivation

When parents bring home a baby, their sleep cycle will be disrupted. Newborns typically wake up every few hours to feed, and this pattern can continue for several months. This means that parents are likely to experience interrupted sleep, waking up multiple times during the night. Additionally, the sleep that parents do get can be lighter and less restful, as they may be listening for their baby and attending to their needs.

Research has shown that new parents experience a significant decrease in the duration and quality of their sleep in the first few months after a baby is born. For first-time parents, this can be even more difficult. One study revealed that 68 per cent of surveyed people were getting seven or more hours of sleep per night prior to having a baby, but afterwards, only 10 per cent of parents were hitting that mark.[8]

There are differences between men and women. After the baby is born, men lose an average of thirteen minutes' sleep per night, while women lose over an hour.[9] Parents' sleep often does not return to pre-pregnancy levels until the youngest child is six years old. This can lead to exhaustion, irritability and difficulty with concentration or memory.

Given how important it is for parents to prioritise their own sleep, grandparents can make a substantial contribution by offering to mind the baby or toddler or an older sibling so the parents can catch a few zeds. New parents should be encouraged to seek support from partners, family members or healthcare professionals to ensure that they are getting enough rest while caring for their baby. This may include taking turns with feedings and other responsibilities, taking naps during the day, or seeking outside help from a postpartum doula or other support services.

So the takeaway for new grandparents at this time is to keep lines of communication open, have clear expectations, respect the new parents' boundaries, and have compassion and thoughtfulness for the new parents, especially in the period around the birth and soon afterwards. Consciously put your own needs as a grandparent second, and navigate the line of being supportive and helpful without being intrusive.

In the next chapter, we'll look at how grandparents can best support their children and grandchildren in the first few years of the youngest generation's life.

The unflinching honesty of grandchildren

David Williamson AO

Dramatist and playwright

The most endearing and sometimes jolting thing about young grandchildren is their unflinching honesty. Whereas adults have instinctively learned long ago that tact and the occasional white lie are necessary survival tactics in the social arena, our young grandchildren don't feel bound by any such restriction.

Quite a few years back, I was driving my second wife of many years' standing, Kristin, and our then little granddaughters Audrey, seven, and Lily, four. The two of them had just come back from a visit to my first wife, Carol. We heard Lily ask Audrey why they had so many grandmothers. Audrey replied, 'Granddad David used to be married to Granny Carol, but then Granny Kristin stole him off her.' Kristin wasn't impressed at this version of family folklore.

Some years back, I directed my actor son Felix, as part of a stellar cast, in the Sydney production of my play *Cruise Control.* During rehearsals, Felix made it clear he was less than impressed with my directorial skills. His young daughter Stella, seven, bounced into our apartment after visiting the set of the play earlier that afternoon. She smiled brightly and said, 'Daddy told me you're a good writer but a lousy director.' Felix went bright red with embarrassment. I told my granddaughter that I couldn't be too bad, as the production had got great crits and her father had been singled out for his performance.

Kristin was singing a goodnight lullaby to our little grandson Banjo when he was not yet four and noticed he was staring at her face. She asked him if something was wrong. 'Granny,' he said, 'you've got very old lips.' She asked what he thought she could do about it. He thought deeply and then said, 'Lip balm.'

It had been a while since my last haircut and trim, and when I picked up young Audrey, who was then only four, she stared intently at my face and declared gravely, 'You're really nice, Granddad, but your eyebrows are awful.' I now go to the barber more often.

On another bedtime talk with a young grandson, he showed Kristin his wallet, which had quite a few high-denomination banknotes in it. She asked him where he got them, and he proudly confessed that he used to sneak into Daddy and Mummy's room when they were asleep and take them out of his father's wallet. She said that was very clever of him but perhaps he should give them back.

We took seven of our fourteen grandchildren to the zoo some years ago, and it was a wild ride trying to corral them all without losing any. At the end of this mini nightmare, we rated them all on their behaviour. We gave Ruby and Mila ten out of ten, and it went down from there.

Before we could get to him, young Atticus, then seven, said glumly, 'I know, I was only three.' His estimate was a tad pessimistic, but it wasn't far off.

As they say, 'From the mouths of babes . . .'

FOUR

Getting to know your grandchild

As I chatted with grandparents while researching this book, it was evident to me that the bond between a grandchild and their grandparent is unique. It's characterised by unbridled love, and an uplifting affection that's apparent to anyone who sees it. Perhaps it is the only family relationship in which people are infatuated with one another simply because they're upright and breathing.

Grandparents can make for some of the best teachers in the world. They love their grandchildren unconditionally, overlook the mistakes for which they would have taken their own children to task, and have a wealth of experience that they want to share.

Human cultures with involved grandparents experience less infant and childhood mortality, as grandparents often provide financial and emotional resources that improve their family's quality of life. But this effect has also been seen in the animal kingdom. Even among orcas!

ORCA GRANDMOTHERS

In December 2019, a marine biologist called Stuart Nattrass from the University of York published a landmark research paper in the *Proceedings of the National Academy of Sciences.* The study found that grandmother killer whales (or orcas) helped improve their grandcalves' chances of survival, particularly when food was scarce. The southern resident orcas of the Pacific Northwest live in close-knit family units of up to 40 individuals, and the study showed that a calf's risk of death rose significantly for two years following the death of its grandmother. Because orca societies are matriarchal, it's likely that these older females carry with them crucial knowledge about food resources that can mean life or death for their kin.

Everybody benefits

Grandchildren who enjoy a strong bond with cluey, involved, caring grandparents develop higher self-esteem and better emotional and social skills, and have fewer emotional problems, including depression.[1] They have an ability to withstand peer pressure and show enhanced academic performance and better behavioural adjustment.[2]

At the same time, grandparents seem to derive countless advantages from having a close relationship with their grandchildren. Grandparents who care for their grandchildren have less stress and better socialisation, are more physically active, and live longer, on average, than grandparents who do not.[3] Caring for grandchildren is also associated with better executive function and a reduction in the risk of developing Alzheimer's disease.[4] Another study, published in the *Proceedings of the Royal Society*, found that grandmothers may feel a deeper emotional connection to their grandchildren than to their own children.[5]

A strong relationship between a grandchild and a grandparent does not happen automatically. It takes time and effort, and requires support from the child's parents. This chapter will give you a step-by-step guide on what, when and how to go about creating this bond, from which everyone benefits. To get to know your grandchild also takes great patience. The Grandparenting Code recommends that your most important job initially is to watch and learn as much as possible. Who is this little person, and what floats their boat?

Can you become a student of their sleeping and dietary habits? Your grandchild's personality will, over time, unfold in front of you. The latest research shows that a child's personality traits in Grade 1, such as verbal fluency (talkativeness), adaptability (coping with new situations) and self-minimising behaviour (being humble), are strong predictors of the traits they will have in adolescence and adulthood.[6]

Getting to know your grandchildren as babies and toddlers can be a magnificent and gratifying experience. Building a relationship at this age requires you to spend time with them by visiting them regularly, helping to care for them and engaging in activities with them. Obviously, this is harder for grandparents who live interstate or overseas, but you can always use technology, such as video calls or messaging apps, to stay connected and build a relationship with your grandchild.

If you are able to spend time with them regularly—reading books together, singing songs or playing with toys—it will help you understand their interests and personality, and learn about their routines, such as their sleep and feeding schedules, so that you can be helpful and supportive. Follow the guidelines suggested later in this chapter on how to play with babies and toddlers.

As long as it's okay with your grandchild's parents, this can also be a great time to capture special moments that you can look back on in the future—but don't share them without permission.

The four-step model

So how do you bond with a grandchild? If you have more than one, you should aim to form a connection with each of them as individuals, spending one-on-one time with them. I suggest four general principles.

1. Find out their 'thing'

Each of your grandchildren is a distinct individual, with their own unique interests and 'islands of competence' (sport, art, music, dance, drama and so on). In my estimation, one of our most significant roles as grandparents is helping our grandchildren with identity formation: discovering who they are and what they are good at. Encouraging and being interested in their 'spark' will pay big dividends. It is all about doing something you love with your grandchild, whether it's gardening, singing, storytelling, games, cooking or something else again. The aim is to intensify the bonds you forged with your grandchild after they were born; you will both reap the joys of those bonds in every succeeding decade of life.

2. Document and record

Use a mobile phone or video camera to record your grandchildren as they engage in milestone moments involving arts, music, dance, drama or sport. This is a really simple way of indicating that you want to be involved in their life—and that you love them! They benefit from your engagement and interest in their lives. However, care does need to be taken not to share pictures or videos of grandchildren without the consent of the child's parents. Sharing pictures may accidentally expose personal information and potentially lead to unwanted attention from strangers, as well as potential embarrassment for your grandchild later in life.

3. Mark special occasions

On birthdays or vacations, plan a day specifically for each child—and give them free rein on activities.

4. Pass on wisdom and skills

When my dad was growing up, he had a great relationship with his family's gardener, who taught him basic car maintenance, gardening, farming and woodworking, which were passed on to me. Skills like these are great things to pass on to grandchildren, as they may not be commonly taught anymore but can be useful and enjoyable nevertheless. Many grandparents interviewed for this book told of their joy in passing on their hobbies or skills, such as playing an instrument or a sport (like golf), and their love of dance or theatre, cooking, fishing or sewing. By sharing their knowledge and experiences, grandparents can help their grandchildren learn new things and develop important life skills. Most grandparents have life lessons because they've lived through trying times. Sharing these lessons with grandchildren can help them build resilience. (More on this in Chapter 8.)

One-on-one time

Many of the grandparents interviewed for this book told me that their grandchildren's behaviour can change significantly when their parents are not with them. Being with a grandparent one-on-one seems to bring out other aspects of children's personalities. Grandparents should try to find ways to get to know their grandkids by themselves, without parents around. Perhaps offer to babysit, or try to schedule playdates.

The Grandparenting Code recommends that, if time and circumstances allow, grandparents should get to know each grandchild individually, and to keep updating what you know about them as they grow older.

Although it may sound odd, I advocate going on individual 'grandpa dates' or 'grandma dates' with just one grandchild at a time—a real one-on-one. This might be as simple as inviting that grandchild to lunch—and asking them to choose the venue. Whether you have one grandchild or twenty, make this a regular habit.

Tell them you want to know as much as you can about them, so you can always be their cheerleader and their helper. Ask them everything from their favourite colour and fast food, to what they think they might be when they grow up. Unless you have a flypaper brain, it may be helpful to have a small notebook where you can record some of the answers to the questions.

Don't sermonise too much during these date discussions. Just ask a lot of questions and listen. As the Dalai Lama once said, 'When you talk, you are only repeating what you already know. But if you listen, you may learn something new.'

I recommend using what psychologists call 'minimal encouragers' to keep them talking. You can say 'really' so many ways and in so many contexts. 'Really!' as in 'Wow!' 'Really?' as in 'Whoa—I never knew that.' 'Really?' as in 'Are you serious?' 'Really!?' as in 'What the heck!' With the appropriate inflection, that one word can keep kids talking and connecting.

Raising grandchildren

As mentioned in the introduction, 3 per cent of grandparents in Australia are the direct carers of their grandchildren. This can be an incredibly rewarding experience, but with the increasing cost of living, providing for the basic needs of children (especially if the grandparents are retired and living on a fixed income) can be a challenge, even though they may be eligible for government financial assistance.

But the strain can be more than just financial. While some grandparents can manage the physical and emotional demands, others experience a decline in their physical health, and the stress of raising children can lead to mental health issues. There are also legal considerations: under the *Family Law Act*, grandparents have the right to seek parenting orders for their grandchildren, but navigating custody or visitation arrangements can be demanding. Managing school can be tricky too, as grandparents might not be familiar with current educational practices and can struggle to cope with school-related and extracurricular activities.

The spoiling dilemma

Some of the grandparents interviewed for this book revealed that a key part of any visit to grandma and grandpa was the inevitable treats. Such traditions can help strengthen the bonds of family and provide a sense of stability, identity and belonging. Depending on what the treat is, the act of giving can play an important role in preserving the values and cultural heritage of a family, and can help create lasting memories that are cherished for years to come. I still remember how my great aunt, whom I'd see annually when I was a child, always made me Vanillekipferl—a small, crescent-shaped biscuit that originated from Vienna.

The Grandparenting Code says it is the inalienable right of any grandparent to spoil their grandchild, but also urges consultation and moderation. There is a dilemma here. Most grandparents want to show their love and affection for their grandchildren by showering them with gifts and treats. While this can strengthen the bond between grandparents and grandchildren, it can also create grandchildren who believe that grandparental gifts are their prerogative. This can make it harder for parents to establish limits and boundaries for their children, and can encourage materialism and even a lack of appreciation for hard work and the value of money.

Here are some Code violations.

Going over the top

Apart from the fact that parents may not have room for an excessive number of items, too many extravagant presents can create a sense of entitlement. For example, the parents might stick to the four-present rule at Christmas (one gift they want, one they need, one they'll wear and one they'll read), but then the grandparents turn up with seven gifts per grandchild.

Crossing the line with age-inappropriate items

Try hard not to gift items that are too old or too young for the grandchild, or things that are incompatible with the child's tastes and interests. One very hip grandmother I know of gave her twelve-year-old grandchild a vibrator!

Giving gifts that are incompatible with the parents' values

Parents of primary-aged children may seek to avoid exposing them to video games, movies, toy guns and toys with a strong gender bias, and grandparents should respect this position. For example, buying a six-year-old grandchild whose parents have a no-screens policy a Nintendo Switch loaded with games would inevitably cause conflict. And with food allergies and intolerances increasingly common these days, grandparents should always check with the parents before giving children edible treats.

In the end, the most important thing is to prioritise the health and wellbeing of the grandchildren and to act in their best interests, and the people with the ultimate responsibility for these are (in most cases) their parents.

As your grandkids get into their mid- and late teens, you should aim to transition to being a consultant or a non-judgemental adviser, and perhaps a financial supporter for education and other worthwhile pursuits. We'll cover how to adjust your grandparenting style when this period arrives in Chapter 7.

Being a consultant

Tell your grandkids what a consultant is, and that your door is always open to them, in person or online. Make sure they understand that you will love it when they ask you for help or for advice of any kind. Tell them you know their parents are always their first advisers and supporters, but that you are the backup. And be clear that you always want to know what's going on in their lives, because the more you know, the more helpful you can be.

Being a long-distance grandparent makes face-to-face grandparent dates challenging, if not impossible. Our increasingly mobile society means that there may be hours of flying time between grandparents and grandchildren. If you don't live close enough to your grandchildren to have regular dates, try to whittle out some one-on-one time when you are visiting the family, or if they are visiting you. In between times, you can always hop on Skype, Zoom, Teams, Google Chat or FaceTime with them.

Familiarise yourself with whichever communication or social-media platforms the family uses, whether it's Facebook,

Instagram, Snapchat or WhatsApp. If it is all too confusing, remember you can always use text messages or the phone.

And while the family may have gone high-tech, the Grandparenting Code suggests that you can go 'old school' by writing your grandchild a card or letter. A handwritten card shows effort, thoughtfulness and a personal touch that a digital message cannot convey. And unlike online communications, handwritten letters can become cherished objects for the future. Birthday cards written on real stationery with an old-fashioned fountain pen may be the only piece of 'snail mail' they ever get! Handwritten communications can be a formidable tool to have in your grandparenting toolbox.

Whatever connection methods you choose, remember that the deepest and most lasting personal relationships form and are cemented one-on-one!

Conflict between a grandchild and their parents

Being a grandparent is not all bunny rabbits and rainbows; conflicts can arise between grandchildren and their parents and you may get dragged in. Handling a conflict between a grandchild and their parents can be challenging for a grandparent, as they may feel torn between supporting their grandchild and respecting the parents' authority. The Grandparenting Code argues that your job as a grandparent is to try to understand the perspective of both sides and avoid taking sides or judging. Communicate with your grandchild and their parent in a respectful and calm manner, and listen to their concerns and feelings. Above all, avoid getting involved in the conflict unless you are asked to or it is necessary for the safety or wellbeing of your grandchild. In other words, you have to respect the rules and decisions of the parent, even if you disagree with them, unless they are harmful or abusive to your grandchild.

A serious and prolonged battle between a grandchild and their parents is a tough situation for grandparents to navigate. These altercations can manifest in different ways and be triggered by different things, but they often boil down to a disagreement between parties due to strong differences in opinions, interests and values. More often than not, family members in conflict lose their sophistication and become emotionally immature.

Here are some tips on how grandparents can approach this situation:

- The Grandparenting Code advises grandparents to remain neutral, as taking sides can intensify the conflict and damage relationships. Try to listen to both sides and avoid making judgements. (There are exceptions to this rule, which are outlined in the Grandparenting Code itself; see pages 229–30.)

- Encourage the grandchild and their parents to talk to each other and to try to resolve the conflict. Suggest that they express their feelings in a calm and respectful way, and that they listen to each other's perspectives.
- Respect the boundaries set by the parents, even if you don't agree with them. Grandparents should not try to undermine the parents' authority, or take actions that could escalate the conflict.
- If the conflict persists or intensifies, it might be helpful to seek the assistance of a family therapist or mediator. A trained professional can help facilitate communication and resolution of the conflict in a neutral and constructive manner.

When grandparents have to intervene

While in an ideal world we would simply allow the parents to do all the parenting, there may be times when grandparents need to intervene.

Although most of us have accumulated some valuable child-rearing experience over the years, our wisdom is not always welcome. Sharing it can elicit a negative response, especially if the grandchild's parents sense disapproval and/or judgement. Deciding whether to speak up or not is complex, but the Grandparenting Code argues that there are just a few circumstances when silence is counterproductive and grandparents have a duty of care to act.

Disrespect

As in all relationships, you're entitled to set boundaries for the way people treat you. Assuming there's no diagnosed mental illness involved, if your grandchild uses foul language in your presence, or is bad-mannered towards you or others, you should speak up. An appropriate response might be a firm 'It's not okay to talk to me like that', but it's best to leave any disciplinary action to the parents.

The Grandparenting Code encourages you to let the parents know about your grandchild's behaviour when the child is not in the room, and give them any necessary details. Encourage the parents to deal with the issue privately. A public reprimand risks humiliating or embarrassing the child and damaging their self-esteem. Instead, it's better for the parents to have a private conversation with the child in a calm and supportive environment. This will allow the child to feel heard and understood, and afford them the opportunity to understand and learn from their mistakes.

If the behaviour is particularly dangerous or disruptive, it may be necessary for you to address it in the moment, but it's still important to maintain a calm and supportive manner that helps the child learn and grow.

Developmental delays

Sometimes parents are too close to their children to notice when there might be something wrong. Grandparents have raised children before, and so will often know what to look for when it comes to a child's development. If you have any concerns, talk to the child's parents and share any observations you have made. It may be that they have noticed the same things. Encourage them to consult a healthcare professional. If a diagnosis of a developmental delay is ultimately made, educate yourself about the specific details of the condition, and about the resources available to help the child and their family.

It's important to remember that early intervention and treatment can make a big difference in the outcome for children with developmental delays, so it's vital to act promptly and get the right support. (For more on this see Chapter 11, on grandparenting neurodiverse children.)

Safety

To me, this is a no-brainer. If you have legitimate concerns about the health and wellbeing of your grandchild, you need to speak up. Examples of safety issues include substance abuse, bullying, internet safety (especially cyberbullying), road safety (bike helmets), and any reasonable suspicion of physical, emotional or sexual abuse.

When and how to talk with the parents

Find the right circumstances that will allow you to discuss these concerns with your adult child and/or their partner. Preferably, choose a moment when your grandkids are not in the room, set out your concerns and offer to help develop an action plan.

If the parents show no interest but you remain concerned, you might decide to discuss the issue with a GP or a school welfare team member. If you feel there is a serious risk to the child's safety or wellbeing, then you must call the police—although don't expect to be thanked by the parents for that.

Harmony Central

In a close grandparent–grandchild relationship, everyone wins. The research suggests that having close relationships with grandchildren can improve grandparents' mental health and reduce their risk of depression and cognitive decline in older age. If you are actively involved in your grandchildren's lives, you'll likely have better physical health, including a lower risk of cardiovascular disease, and higher levels of life satisfaction, a greater sense of purpose and greater happiness.

For their part, the grandchildren will likely have more emotional support and feel a greater sense of security, will be happier and more confident, and will have higher self-esteem. They will tend to do better in school and have greater educational success due to the additional support, guidance and encouragement they are receiving.

Grandparents can provide a unique perspective on life, and their experiences and insights can broaden children's understanding of the world. Children who have close relationships with their grandparents often have stronger relationships with their parents too, as grandparents can provide them with emotional support and help mediate conflicts. They also tend to have better coping skills and to be more resilient in the face of adversity.

The credibility of the grandparents can be cemented early on by being actively involved in the lives of their grandchildren. Many grandparents wonder how this might be done. The answer lies in play. Play is not just a natural way for children to learn about and explore the world around them, but it also boosts their creativity; facilitates coping, mastery, self-expression, achievement and learning; and is vital to a child's optimal growth and development. The next chapter examines the advantages of playing with grandchildren from an early age, with practical examples for different age groups.

FIVE
The power of play

If, like me, you are interested in how children develop and wonder what sort of grandchild you are going to end up with—and, more importantly, if you can influence the outcome in any way—read on! The nursery rhyme may have told us that little boys were made of 'frogs and snails and puppy dogs' tails' and little girls were 'sugar and spice and all things nice', but that's not true. In fact, it's a lot more complicated.

What determines your grandchild's personality?

The truth is that your grandchild's personality and disposition will be determined by a combination of factors, including the

23 chromosomes they inherit from their mum and the 23 they inherit from their dad, and the genetic 'roll of the dice' that determines what genetic information passes from parents to offspring. To put it simply, your grandchild will have a unique combination of genes inherited from their parents, and these genes will influence their physical and behavioural characteristics. Some traits, such as height or eye colour, are determined by a single gene, while others, such as their susceptibility to certain diseases, are influenced by multiple genes working together. Additionally, certain personality traits and dispositions may be more likely to develop based on your grandchild's genetic make-up.

Of course, the environment a child grows up in also plays a substantial role in shaping their personality and disposition, as do their life experiences and interactions with you and others, especially during their first five years.

Remember that your grandchild is born with 86 billion brain cells (neurons), which they will have for the rest of their life,[1] but what really makes their brain hum—and what enables them to function—are the connections between those cells, which are faster in the first five years than at any other time in their life. Babies make an incredible 1 million new neural connections (synapses) every second, and how these wire up is

FUN FACTS ABOUT YOUR NEWBORN GRANDCHILD

- Babies are born with no kneecaps.[2]
- They have no tears.[3]
- They are born with 300 bones—50 per cent more bones than adults have.[4]
- Eighty per cent of them have a birthmark.[5]
- Their hair falls out during the first few weeks after birth.[6]
- They have impressive reflexes at birth.[7]
- They start to smile sometime between six and eight weeks of age.[8]
- They already know their mother's taste in music.[9]
- They laugh 300 to 400 times a day (compared to 15–20 times per day for adults).[10]
- They have three times the number of tastebuds as adults.[11]

crucial to the development of the child's social skills, personality, cognitive skills, decision-making, ability to concentrate and behaviour.[12]

The learning machine

Your grandchild is a learning machine—they are born ready to learn, and their brains develop through use. The connections wire up through their everyday experiences: the amount and quality of the care, stimulation and interaction they receive in their first days, weeks, months and years determine which brain connections develop and will last for a lifetime.

Early in their life, your grandchild will make 'bids' to engage with you—by cooing, smiling and crying. As their brain matures, these bids become more sophisticated, and they are able to communicate their needs and interests more precisely. Each of these little bids is an opportunity for you as a grandparent to be either responsive or unresponsive to the child's needs.

This neurological ping-pong is fundamental to the wiring of the child's brain. The grandparent who pays attention and responds to and interacts with their grandchild is literally building the child's brain. That's why it's so important to talk, sing, read and play with children from the day they're born, and to provide them with a clean, safe and protected physical environment while they are playing and learning.

There is no doubt that some grandparents are eager to play a role in providing their young grandchild with such an environment, while others are not. Some might be retired, planning to retire, travelling or thinking about it, or just looking forward to having more time for themselves and/or their partner. Grandparents may be running half-marathons or may not be in great health, and so might have limits on the energy they can expend on others.

Your role as a grandparent will depend on what you want to do, what you can do and how your grandchild's parents feel about your capacity to care for their offspring.

Consider your needs

Especially in the first five crucial years of a child's life, the Grandparenting Code requires you to reflect on this new role and consider your own needs and preferences, as well as those of your extended family, and then decide what your level of involvement will be.

It can be helpful to communicate your ability or inability to provide childcare to the grandchild's parents. This may require a courageous conversation in which you are clear and firm about the specific times you are available to provide such care, and set boundaries around the types of tasks or responsibilities you are comfortable taking on.

It's also important to make time for your own needs and responsibilities outside of childcare. This is especially important if you are already a carer yourself, if you have other grandchildren or if you have other commitments. In most instances, how available you can be to this small child will be contingent on a raft of practical and emotional considerations, including geography, transport, and your health and mobility.

The Code states that it is essential for you to decide on how much energy you choose to expend as a grandparent—and to be flexible, because life circumstances change. Jane Caro's contribution to this book (see pages 87–8) expresses her admiration for her daughter's patience and capacity to play Lego with her child, and acknowledges that this was not her own strong suit as a parent. Clearly communicating your boundaries to your grandchild's parents will set realistic expectations and help avoid disappointment or even conflict.

If you feel you'd like to be involved and the grandchild's parents are up for it, then the Code advises that play is the best way to build a relationship with your young grandchild. The problem is that as we get older, taking time to play can feel embarrassing or silly, even a pointless waste of time—almost a diversion from 'real' work and life. But as developmental psychologists know, play is anything but trivial. As Maria Montessori said, 'play is the work of the child'.

Play is a crucial part of development

Animal studies, ranging from dolphins to dogs, reveal that play is a near-universal feature of mammalian life.[13] And children will always play, irrespective of whether they live in a rural or an urban environment, or even in a war zone or concentration camp.[14]

FUN FACTS ABOUT PLAY

- Play makes your grandchild physically stronger.[15]
- Play makes your grandchild smarter.[16]
- Play helps your grandchild solve problems.[17]
- Play boosts creativity.[18]
- Play reduces stress.[19]
- Play helps your grandchild make friends.[20]
- Play builds resilience.[21]

Our urge to play is hardwired below the cortex, in the brainstem, which controls functions basic to the survival of all animals, such as heart rate, breathing, digesting food, and sleeping.[22] It is the lowest, most primitive area of the human brain. Scientists have observed the behaviour of small mammals that lack a cortex: they play just as actively as their peers with an intact cortex, proving that the areas of the brain that initiate and sustain vigorous early play are located in subcortical areas of the brain.

The amazing thing is that your grandchild's brain parallels the structure of the brains of those little lab rats: their desire to play originates in the same survival areas of the brain.[23] Play allows their cortex to form the neural pathways that determine how emotionally stable they will be and how easily they will learn. Young children who have inadequate or unsafe play spaces and equipment, an over-structured routine (including too many organised sports, and not enough time for free choice) or a high consumption of technology (including viewing and gaming) may struggle to relate to others and learn from their life experiences.

Playing with babies

In the first few weeks of life, babies seem so minute and delicate. First-time parents are typically laser-focused on getting them fed, changed and sleeping. After those first few weeks, the baby will stay awake a little longer, and parents begin to wonder how to play with their newborn.

Given their own experience in raising children, grandparents are in a great position to show parents (if they are interested) how to incorporate activities that might aid in the baby's development and keep them busy during awake times. Developmental psychologists argue that it is never too early to start playing with the little bundle of joy, and a demo from grandma or grandpa can go down a treat.

Here are some ideas for play with very young babies. (Remember to always supervise the baby while they are playing, and never leave them unattended.)

- *Tummy time*: Place your grandchild on their tummy for short periods of time, gradually increasing the duration. This helps them develop their neck and back muscles, and gives them an opportunity to explore their surroundings.

- *Singing and talking*: Babies love to hear your voice. Sing songs, recite nursery rhymes or talk to the baby, which also helps with their language development.
- *Sensory toys*: Provide your grandchild with toys that stimulate their senses. They love soft toys, rattles and really colourful playthings.
- *Mirrors*: Babies are a little like the Kardashians—they love to look at themselves in the mirror. Hold the baby in front of a mirror and let them explore their reflection.
- *Peekaboo*: This classic game can be great fun for the baby. Cover your face with your hands and then reveal your face while saying 'peekaboo'. This also helps develop your grandchild's sense of object permanence.

Playing with toddlers and young children

Comedy writer Ian Martin sums this up beautifully:

> My parents' generation always said that the best thing about being grandparents is that 'You can hand them back.' Do people still say that? Anyway, it's not. The best bit comes just

> after they've arrived to be coddle-minded. You shut the front door with the usual wafted reassurances to one of your adult children, clasp your hands together like an earnest supply teacher and say, 'So, what do you fancy doing?' What they fancy doing when they're young is tipping 100 balls down the stairs and then laughing at your feigned surprise and outrage. Then, when you're collecting the balls from all over the house, they yawn and ask for juice, so you get them a drink and eventually present them with 85 balls. You do it again, they shriek with excitement for the three whole seconds of plastic avalanche. Rinse, repeat. Exhausting but engaging.[24]

As they get older, children's play becomes more sophisticated. So how do you play with a grandchild of four or five years of age?

- *Board games*: These can be a great way to teach your grandchild about taking turns, following rules and problem-solving. Favourites for young children include Snakes and Ladders and Ludo.
- *Outdoor games*: Toddlers and young children have a lot of energy and love to run through a sprinkler and play outside. Try playing tag or hide and seek, or blowing bubbles or having a picnic.

- *Arts and crafts*: Encourage your grandchild's creativity by providing them with painting or drawing supplies, and building materials such as playdough and Lego.
- *Books*: Reading with your grandchild is a great way to bond and develop their literacy skills. Take trips to the library and read books together, and talk about the story and characters.
- *Role-play*: Young children love to use their imagination. You can join in by pretending to be different characters and imagining fun scenarios.

And don't hesitate to let your toddler grandchild play on their own sometimes—it's more than okay to encourage them to think up their own activities.

What about older grandchildren?

When they reach eight or ten, your grandchild will love to run, cycle, skate, jump on trampolines, swim and play sports. Depending on your own energy levels, you can watch or join in. They might enjoy team sports or individual activities, or be more into art, music, crafts, reading or getting out in nature. The options at this age really are endless. Visit your local science museum together, bake a loaf of bread, build and launch a model rocket.

Here are some more tips on things to do with an older grandkid:

- *More complex board games and card games*: Try Monopoly, Cluedo, Uno, Go Fish and Rummy—although I personally draw the line at poker, which involves gambling and is not appropriate for children.
- *Video games*: Many ten-year-olds enjoy playing video games. You can join in and play games with them, or let them teach you about their favourites.
- *Sports*: Ten-year-olds are becoming more coordinated and athletic. You can play games like basketball, soccer or cricket together, or simply practise throwing and catching a ball.
- *Arts and crafts*: Many ten-year-olds love creative activities. You can make friendship bracelets, draw or paint pictures, or create a scrapbook together.
- *Cooking or baking*: Preparing food together is a great way to spend time together and develop life skills. Try making a fun meal or baking a dessert with your grandchild, and enjoy the fruits of your labour afterwards. Who says buttered white toast and two Mini-Magnums isn't technically a sandwich?

Remember to let your grandchild take the lead on what you do together. Playful and engaging interactions with your grandchild can strengthen your relationship and help them develop important skills.

And keep in mind that we don't need to actively entertain kids 24/7. Play that is too structured or that involves too much grandparent intervention is counterproductive, because children can't develop the skills they need if they are continually being organised and limited. If you allow grandchildren to play on their own terms, they grow in resilience and independence, and build their creativity and problem-solving and risk-management skills.

The beauty of board games

When I was growing up, board games provided an opportunity for my family to spend quality time together and engage in some fun and entertaining bonding. Evidence says that games like these help children improve their cognitive function and develop social skills such as problem-solving, strategic and critical thinking, and teamwork.[25]

Long-distance grandparents can take advantage of the fact that many of these games (including Monopoly, Scrabble, Chess, Snakes and Ladders, and Uno) are now available online as smartphone or tablet apps. Some are free, while others must be paid for. Before you suggest online board games to your grandchildren, check with their parents so they can preview each app and give their permission.

GREAT BOARD GAMES FOR GRAND-PARENTS AND GRANDCHILDREN

The most popular board games vary by country and region, but some of the best known and most widely played board games globally include:

1. Chess
2. Monopoly
3. Scrabble
4. Risk
5. Clue (also known as Cluedo)
6. The Settlers of Catan (also known as Catan)
7. Go
8. Backgammon
9. Pictionary
10. Checkers (also known as Draughts)

The Grandparenting Code suggests that without play and physical activity, your grandchild can't cultivate the skills necessary to handle changing times. For your own sake and the sake of your grandchildren, embrace play with exuberance and give it the place it deserves in our lives.

In the words of the educational thinker Friedrich Fröbel: 'Play is the highest expression of human development in childhood, for it alone is the free expression of what is in a child's soul.'

There is a threat to play on the developmental horizon in the form of screens and screentime. As your grandchild grows, screens will be something you as a grandparent will need to deal with. The next chapter offers some clear advice on this topic.

What your grandchildren (and their parents) teach you

Jane Caro AM

Writer, social commentator and novelist

When I became a parent, I quickly realised that, far from me teaching my children very much, the boot was firmly on the other (small) foot. I learned more about myself—about my weaknesses, my failings, my vulnerabilities and my petty selfishness—than I have at any other time. However, I also learned more about my ability to endure, my capacity for patience, my ability to operate on virtually no sleep and my doggedness than I had ever thought possible.

My daughters not only showed me who I was, they made me into the person I have become.

I am now watching my elder daughter (along with my son-in-law) parent my two grandchildren. My younger daughter is twelve weeks pregnant as I write this, so we are excitedly awaiting another addition to the family.

My daughter's patience with her children is something I admire greatly. She plays games with them—something I avoided like the plague! I'd sing songs, tell stories, read books and take them to visit family and friends till the cows came home, but play cafes? Or Barbies? Or build Lego? No way. I won't even do it with my adored grandchildren. I'll play Snap, Go Fish or Concentration (my four-year-old granddaughter wipes the floor with me), even Junior Monopoly if pushed, but that is it.

Fortunately, a lifetime of creative writing has come in handy. My daughter calls me the jukebox of stories, and I have learned much about the power of episodes and cliffhangers from watching how they keep my grandchildren enthralled.

My daughter makes sure her children eat well—something I struggled with and mostly failed at when my own girls were small—and she also ensures they pack as much fun into a day as possible. I love that. She isn't a perfect parent by any means (thank goodness—imagine how damaging that would be to a real, human child), but it's those moments when I may not completely agree with what she is doing that have taught me the most of all.

Namely, how very important it is for Grandma to keep her mouth shut.

SIX
Screentime

In 91 per cent of homes in Australia, there is a powerful force competing for your grandchild's attention, a pixeled portal to so many adventures.[1] If it's not a smartphone or tablet, it is a gaming console. Infants, toddlers and preschoolers are now growing up in environments saturated with a variety of traditional and new technologies. Chances are your grandchild already plays with one. Many of my youngest clients want one thing more than anything else: to watch a show or play a video game. Digital devices and the software they use have become the undisputed champions of the toy kingdom (whether we like it or not).

The phrase 'screentime', although in common usage, covers a wide range of activities. When it comes to your grandchildren, their 'screen' can be anything from a desktop computer for their homework to an iPad for video gaming, or a Kindle for reading. Since most displays today have many functions, any conversation about screens will be hazy unless we specifically identify the content, context and linkages associated with particular screen-centred activities.

In this chapter I will endeavour to cover the full range of technology that your grandchildren may use or have exposure to—including free-to-air TV; streaming services such as Stan, Netflix and Disney+; internet video such as YouTube; phone and tablet games; and gaming consoles such as Nintendo Switch, PlayStation and Xbox.

The American Academy of Pediatrics advises limiting older children's screentime to no more than one or two hours per day and avoiding screens for babies younger than eighteen to 24 months, unless they are video chatting with relatives.[2]

They point out that the harmful impacts of excessive screen usage include weight gain, sleep troubles and behavioural disorders. It is important for grandparents to monitor their grandchild's screentime and to make sure that the content they are viewing is high-quality and engaging. As responsible, caring adults, grandparents should also set screentime rules and agree on consequences for breaking them, and encourage their grandchild to engage in active, creative play.

Depending on your grandchild's age, the digital distractions on offer will come in a variety of flavours: shows like *Peppa Pig* and *Bluey* and games like *Fortnite*, *Minecraft*, *Apex Legends*, *Grand Theft Auto*, *FIFA*, *NBA 2K23* and many more. The boffins who count these things claim that these games are played by 8.6 million households in Australia, and there is a fear that excessive screentime could make activities such as reading, colouring in, baking or watching movies together obsolete.

With screens virtually everywhere, controlling a grandchild's screentime can be challenging. How much is too much? How can you manage your grandchild's screentime? How will you know if your grandchildren are addicted to screens?

FACTS ABOUT VIDEO GAMING IN AUSTRALIA

- There are 5.5 million households with two or more gaming devices.
- 8.6 million Australian households play video games.
- 17 million Australians play video games.
- The average age of a video-game player is 35.

- Australians play video games for an average of 83 minutes a day.
- 76 per cent of parents play video games with their children.
- 36 per cent of players have made friends through video gaming.
- 70 per cent of parents say that they are familiar with parental controls.
- 60 per cent of parents say that they set the rules for video gaming.
- 60 per cent of children say that they learn with video games at school.[3]

Not all screentime is the same

It's important to understand that not all screentime is created equal. There are many studies that suggest that screentime in moderation can have positive effects. Technology, when used in a safe, smart and responsible way, can take away physical barriers to social connections, which can be important for children who find it hard to make friends or who have special interests or special needs. It also improves access to information, enhances learning experiences, helps with the development of technical skills, increases creativity, provides access to online resources and improves problem-solving skills. So it is not all bad.

What is the likelihood that your grandchild will have access to a screen? Statistics from 2020 reveal that just under half (46 per cent) of Australian children aged six to thirteen used a mobile phone, up from 41 per cent in 2015.[4] If they are in secondary school, most will have their own tablet or mobile phone. No wonder excessive screentime topped a list of parents' concerns in a 2021 poll by The Royal Children's Hospital Melbourne.[5]

What's a reasonable amount of screentime?

First things first. How many hours should your grandchild spend with a screen? The Australian eSafety Commission—the world's first government agency dedicated to keeping people safer online—argues that there is no magic figure. Instead, they suggest that any determination of the optimal amount of screentime should take into account the child's age and maturity, the content they are looking at, their learning needs, and the amount of sleep and exercise they get.[6]

What the eSafety Commission is saying is that rather than just focus on the clock, we also need to consider what children are doing with their screentime, as well as our own involvement.

Some researchers worry that grandparents are waving the white flag on this issue. They are concerned that grandparents may in fact be fuelling excessive device usage among their grandchildren, which is contributing to growing mental and physical health issues worldwide.[7]

The Grandparenting Code argues that if, in your judgement, your grandchild's screentime is interfering with their face-to-face connections with their family and friends, and/or with their sleep and exercise, then limits should be set.

What—or who—determines your grandchild's use?

Your grandchildren's use of technology will largely be the result of the limits and boundaries set at home. The Code advises that, while you should consider their parents' approach, when your grandchildren are in your care, it is absolutely your right to decide what is okay and what isn't as far as screentime goes. Some grandparents I have talked to freely admit to letting their grandchildren engage in activities that they know their parents would never permit: too much chocolate or ice-cream, flexible bedtimes and excessive screentime. They like to spoil their grandchildren. But it is your job, in consultation with the child's parents, to set time limits and content rules for your grandchildren.

In 2019, researchers from Ben Gurion University in Israel set out to discover what factors increased the likelihood of excessive screen usage by children. They found that while the children in the sample were with their grandparents, they spent about half their time looking at a mobile phone, tablet, computer or television.[8] Whether this was an attempt by grandparents to bond with the children, keep them entertained or show love and affection, or a lack of knowledge or experience, is not clear from the research.

Although there is nothing inherently wrong with children using screens while in the care of grandparents (especially if their grandparents are playing with them), all technology should be used in moderation and in a safe and supervised manner, as excessive screentime can have negative effects on children's health and development.

Research has shown that too much screentime can lead to a variety of issues, including obesity, sleep problems, behavioural problems and a decline in cognitive and social-emotional development. In addition, especially when they involve highly stimulating activities, some games can activate the brain's reward system and release dopamine, a neurotransmitter associated with pleasure and motivation. This can create a cycle of seeking more screentime to experience the same pleasurable effects.

So the Grandparenting Code suggests that it is important for grandparents to monitor their grandchildren's screentime and make sure they are engaging in a variety of activities, including physical play, socialising with peers and reading. They can also encourage activities such as arts and crafts, cooking and outdoor exploration, to promote healthy development.

Designate set periods for play, reading a book, napping or quiet time. All grandchildren will benefit from having a designated time limit for screen usage—you must and should set one. We teach kids how to treat us, and your grandkids need to know that you say what goes on in your house. In essence, you set the agenda.

The Grandparenting Code maintains that grandparents ought to be teaching their grandchildren about responsible screentime by controlling their media use. You can do this by setting simple rules on screentime when you are babysitting. Use some of the time you spend with your grandchildren to fuel their interest in the real world. It is fair and reasonable to have rules about phone/tablet/TV time, board-game time and food consumption time—although not all grandparents are averse to snacking 24 hours a day!

So it's time to get empowered and informed. I am a fan of YouTube Kids, a spinoff of YouTube. This is a separate app that is available in most smartphone, tablet and television app stores, which offers videos for children in a safer version of the regular YouTube app. But be warned! It is not 100 per cent safe, so there's a possibility that they could be exposed to nudity, violence and promotions for junk food. You need to remain vigilant about what your grandchildren are watching.

A study of the YouTube Kids app by Common Sense Media notes that 27 per cent of YouTube videos watched by children aged eight and under were actually intended for older audiences, with violence being the most common negative content type.[9] Visit www.commonsensemedia.org for tips on making YouTube safe, and to read reviews of movies and TV shows that children may be interested in.

Disney+, Netflix and YouTube all offer an intoxicating variety of watchable shows. I rarely encounter children who can self-regulate in the face of such a televisual banquet. If you still have a DVD or Blu-ray player, my advice is to use that instead. Why? A DVD has a start and finish, whereas streaming services are bottomless pits in which the next episode or show cues up automatically.

If streaming services are your only option, then I suggest you establish restrictions for your grandchildren. Set a time limit, or have a policy of watching only two shows in a row, or the YouTube top three. This can help diminish the possibility of your grandchildren binge-watching for hours. Once they reach the agreed limit, it is time for an alternative activity—spending time in the kitchen or the garden, playing a ball game outdoors, feeding the dog or helping with a chore.

Is there such a thing as an internet addiction?

There is no doubt that video games have been designed to promise those who play them never-ending entertainment and exhilaration. Experiments with rats show that mammalian brains love intermittent, unexpected rewards, which is exactly what these games offer.[10]

TV poses a similar problem. If you're roughly my age, you probably also liked watching shows like *I Dream of Jeannie*, *Hogan's Heroes* and *Gilligan's Island* when you were young. But we had to endure commercial breaks, the shows couldn't be rewatched on demand, and they all ended after 30 or 60 minutes. Today, streaming services such as Netflix will automatically begin the next episode as soon as the previous one concludes. Likewise, popular video games like *Fortnite Battle Royale* don't have save points, so if kids are playing online with friends, they have to keep going until the game ends. Unless adults enforce limits or create interruptions, kids can stay glued to their screens.

Sometimes, when your grandchild is told that it is time to put the device away, their mood may change and they might exhibit withdrawal symptoms. Young people can become preoccupied with the internet and digital media, to the point that they lose the ability to control the amount of time they spend interfacing with digital technology. No matter what is said or done, and in spite of parents' attempts to intervene, the behaviour continues. It's a Ferrari brain, with bicycle brakes!

Whether or not you should use the word 'addiction' depends on which psychologist you talk to. The concept of internet addiction is a relatively new phenomenon, and there is debate among mental health professionals about whether it should be considered a genuine mental illness.

Some argue that excessive internet use, whether it manifests in gaming, social-media use or binge-watching, can be a symptom of other mental health issues, such as anxiety, depression or obsessive-compulsive disorder. Others maintain that internet addiction should be classified as a distinct disorder, with its own set of diagnostic criteria.

For the record, internet addiction is not currently recognised as a mental illness in the *Diagnostic and Statistical Manual of Mental Disorders* (DSM-5), the standard reference work on mental disorders used by mental health professionals around the world, including in Australia. It does make an appearance in the appendix as a 'condition for further study'. This means that further research is needed to determine whether internet addiction should be included as a formal diagnosable condition in future editions of the DSM.

Even so, there are warning signs to look out for if you are concerned about your grandchildren's screentime.

While every grandchild and every situation is different, if grandparents recognise the signs listed in the following box, or physical, mental or academic problems, they should in the first instance discuss their observations with the child's parents.

SIGNS OF EXCESSIVE SCREEN USE

1. Your grandchild can't control their screen use, in that they have trouble stopping using devices.
2. They lose interest in other activities, such as reading, playing outside or with toys, or taking part in sports.
3. Digital activities preoccupy their thoughts: if they talk incessantly about a video game, wonder what a favourite YouTuber will post next or act out scenes from games, this could be a sign of addiction.
4. Some grandchildren can become argumentative, aggressive or even violent over restrictions on screen use.
5. Your grandchild shows signs of withdrawal when it's time to turn off the TV for bedtime or put away mobile devices.
6. Their tolerance is increasing: they used to watch 30 minutes of YouTube after school each day, but now they are watching it on a phone on the way home from school as well.

7. They're deceptive about their screen use, sneaking a tablet into bed at night or lying about how long they've been playing for.
8. A screen is their mood booster: they need a TV show or game to make them feel better or offer an escape.
9. Children withdraw from socialising with family and friends, preferring to spend time alone with screens. They may avoid or ignore invitations to social events or become irritable or defensive when interrupted.

There are steps you can take to help children overcome excessive screen use.

Set limits: Parents and grandparents should establish clear and consistent rules and boundaries regarding the child's screen use, which are enforced irrespective of which home the child is in. They should limit the amount and type of digital content the child can engage with, as well as the time and place of screen use. They should also monitor the screen-centred activities and enforce consequences for breaking the rules.

Encourage alternatives: Grandparents should encourage their grandchild to engage in other activities that are fun, healthy and rewarding, such as sports, hobbies, art, music or socialising. They should also provide opportunities for their grandchild to participate in family or community events, or to volunteer for a cause.[11]

Communicate and support: Grandparents should communicate with their grandchild in a respectful and empathetic way, and listen to their feelings and concerns. They should avoid criticising, blaming or shaming their grandchild for their dependence on screens. They should also express their love and support for their grandchild, and praise their efforts and achievements in overcoming their problem.

There are technological solutions that can assist grandparents in enforcing the internet-use rules, too. These include router plug-ins, which allow adult carers to control the internet access of different devices in the household. They enable adults to set schedules, limits and filters for each device, and monitor their usage and activity. Some examples of router plug-ins are Circle, KoalaSafe and Torch.

There are also parental-control apps that the adults can install on the child's device or their own device to manage their screentime. They can remotely lock or unlock the device, or send them messages or reminders. Some examples of parental-control apps are Qustodio, OurPact and Screen Time.

Ultimately, if none of these techniques work, then the final solution is to suggest that your grandchild's parents seek professional help. Parents should consult a qualified mental health professional if they suspect their child has an internet or screen addiction. A professional can assess the child's condition, provide a diagnosis and recommend a treatment plan.

Grandsharenting

Another danger with screens is not what children are doing online, but rather what their caregivers are posting. As their beautiful, funny and talented kids grow up it can be very tempting for parents to show off their kids to the world, also known as 'sharenting'—or, in the case of grandparents, 'grandsharenting'. Some grandparents have a habit of sharing private images of or information about children online—on Facebook, for example. Most grandparents doing this have good intentions, of course, but they can be oblivious to the dangers.

One study found that, on average, caregivers post nearly 1500 photos online by a child's fifth birthday. [12] The Australian Federal Police have warned parents not to post photos of their children, especially on their first day of school, without first ensuring that their privacy settings are enabled.[13] One bank in the United Kingdom has predicted that, by 2030, 'sharenting' will account for two-thirds of identity fraud experienced by young people over eighteen, and will cost £667 million ($1.25 billion) per year.[14]

But the dangers of sharenting are not just about identity fraud: paedophiles scour the web to collect identifying photos of children.

The fact is that when anyone posts an image of anything on the web they have lost control over it. Even if they are only sharing the image within a private Facebook group, anyone with access to that private group can take the image and repost it elsewhere. The Grandparenting Code encourages grandparents to celebrate milestone moments, but they must remain mindful of what they do with any photos they take.

Susan McLean, aka the 'cybercop', Australia's foremost cyber-safety expert, urges all grandparents to ensure that their account is 'locked down' to private—and that means friends only. If they ever share a school photo, McLean urges adults to ensure that the image and the logo of the school is blurred, and the photo isn't one that has been taken in an identifiable location, such as at a front door or in the street. Furthermore, she advises, grandparents should be sure that 'location services' are turned off on their smartphone or camera, so that they are not inadvertently embedding metadata including the GPS coordinates of where that photo was taken.

To learn how to stop sharing your location in the photos you take, check the user guide for the model of smartphone you have, or do a Google search.

What can grandparents do?

Things to be aware of around grandsharenting:

- Always check with your grandchild's parents before posting, sharing or tagging images that include their child.
- Avoid sharing photos and videos that contain or reveal a child's personal details, such as their full name, their contact information, or the location of their school or home.
- Don't add comments to photos that might reveal locations, such as the suburb, park or street a photo was taken in, or even identifying it as your own home.

- Make sure that schedules of your grandchildren's activities are never posted online. Only share information with people you really know and trust; never post to all your friends as a group. If sharing images or information on social media, you must be selective and ensure that your privacy settings are switched on.
- Be aware that if a friend likes your picture on Facebook, it may also then become visible to *their* friends.
- Remember that the information and photos you share will be part of your grandchild's digital reputation. It is impossible to completely remove all traces of data online, and some information may still be accessible through data brokers and people-search sites, so it is important to take steps to minimise your grandchild's digital footprint and protect their privacy online, by keeping as much of their personal information as possible off the internet.
- Be mindful about metadata and geolocations: most digital photos contain information about where and when the image was taken. Check the location settings on your phone so that you understand which apps have access to your geolocation.
- Understand that photos and videos posted on social-media sites like Facebook may become the property of the site

owner. Some social-media sites give themselves the right to copy and use your photos and videos, so be aware of the terms and conditions.

Whether to share anything of their grandchild's life online is a challenging issue for many grandparents (and parents). There exists an uncomfortable paradox: sharing images of and information about children may have implications for the children's privacy, but social media may also be an important source of support and connection with family and friends. The answer is to be informed and to tread carefully.

Every moment is teachable

There is no doubt that grandparents play a crucial role in helping their grandchildren develop healthy screen habits. The Grandparenting Code suggests that teaching grandchildren to use technology in a safe, smart and responsible way involves self-educating about the technologies and apps children are using, and the risks associated with them. The eSafety Commissioner's website provides online safety education and resources such as videos, games and lesson plans to help children, young people and adults develop good digital skills and stay safe online.[15]

The Grandparenting Code recognises that screens are here to stay and can offer many positives. It's never too early to develop a screentime plan with your family. Let your children and grandchildren share their ideas and concerns. The Code carries an expectation that grandparents will work with their grandchildren's parents to set screentime boundaries and establish rules around internet use, while simultaneously modelling moderate screentime behaviour themselves. An important aspect is showing an interest in grandchildren's online lives. Offer to play games or watch videos together.

Keep a lookout for news items relating to kids' screen usage, and use these to create teachable moments by drawing your grandchild's attention to the issue. Ask them what they think and correct any misconceptions they might have. This is a powerful way to engage young people in an open conversation about online safety, privacy and responsible internet use.

By taking these steps, grandparents can be a positive influence in their grandchildren's lives, and help them develop healthy screen habits and stay safe online.

Connecting with an older grandchild

Jenny Kee AO

Fashion designer

The key to my relationship with my granddaughter is that it is based on mutual respect, which helps bridge the generation gap and fosters understanding and appreciation. It also builds trust: when grandchildren feel respected by their grandparents, they are more likely to trust them and confide in them, which strengthens the bond and creates a solid foundation for a positive relationship. This is especially important in a grandparent–grandchild relationship where there may be differences in values, beliefs and lifestyles.

Understand that your relationship with a grandchild is different from that with your child, particularly in the level of your involvement. Parents are typically more involved in their children's lives than grandparents, as they are responsible for meeting their children's daily needs, making decisions for them, enforcing rules and providing emotional support. Grandparents, on the other hand, may have a less frequent and more advisory role.

It's important to respect your grandchildren's autonomy and not to interfere—don't give them unsolicited advice. While sharing your life experiences and wisdom can be helpful, it's important to recognise that your grandchildren are their own individuals, with their own unique experiences and perspectives. Allow them to make their own decisions and be there to support them.

Avoid being too critical: criticising or judging your grandchildren's choices can be counterproductive and damaging to your relationship. Instead, try to be supportive and offer constructive feedback when appropriate. It's important to be open-minded when giving advice to your grandchildren. Recognise that they may have different beliefs and values, and that their experiences may be different from yours.

I love to connect with my granddaughter through food preparation. It's a powerful way to bond as it evokes memories, emotions and traditions, and sharing meals creates an experience that builds relationships and fosters a sense of community. Cooking and sharing food is a wonderful way to express your love and care for your grandchild, and, of course, trying new foods and cuisines helps you both explore and discover different cultures and traditions.

Over the years, travelling overseas with my granddaughter has been a delight, a fun and rewarding experience for both of us. The trips we've taken together provide an excellent opportunity for us to create new memories and strengthen our relationship.

Overall, it's this kind of respect that is essential in a grandparent–grandchild relationship. It can help build trust, encourage open communication and positive behaviour, and navigate differences—all of which can lead to a more fulfilling relationship for everyone.

SEVEN

Grandparenting teens

Of all the natural events that occur in the family life cycle, the emergence of adolescence is the one most likely to test a household's flexibility and tolerance. The developmental tasks of teenagers include making friends, emancipating from parents, figuring out their identity and acquiring the skills for future economic independence. Experts in adolescent mental health argue that the journey from childhood to mature adulthood is now more complex and protracted than ever before,[1] as a result of a raft of destabilising social, technological and economic changes in society. The final part of the Grandparenting Code suggests that, for grandparents, the fun does not have to stop when grandchildren hit their teenage years, but the approach does need to be different.

So how can grandparents help their grandchildren navigate this tricky time? Well, the first thing they need is a developmental perspective. Buckle up for a crash course in adolescence.

The developmental psychology of adolescence

While some things about the psychology of teenagers will never change, such as the three big questions of adolescence—Am I normal? Who am I? Where am I going?—other aspects of the journey from childhood to adulthood are quite different from when your own children went through this stage. Theoretically, grandparents are better prepared for this period than parents, as they have lived through it once before.

The first recorded use of the word 'adolescence' appeared in the fifteenth century.[2] The term comes from the Latin word *adolescere*, which means 'to grow up or to grow into maturity'. Adolescence is a unique developmental phase, a period of transition, typically characterised by marked physical, cognitive and emotional changes, as well as a desire for increased autonomy, which helps in the development of their identity.

Your teenage grandchildren are no longer children, nor are they yet adults—and therein lies the problem. They are striving for independence and autonomy, yet they are still fragile beings in the process of growing and developing.

The physical changes of adolescence

In childhood, growth is slow and steady, but at puberty the teenager changes rapidly and dramatically, as hormones start coursing through their body. Some children can experience dramatic growth spurts in their adolescent years—becoming up to ten centimetres taller in a year, and gaining between nine and thirteen kilograms—so adults need to be tolerant when food or drink is spilt, as they become less coordinated. Early adolescents tend to be self-conscious about their physical appearance, and this anxiety can be exacerbated by Instagram, Snapchat, TikTok and the like: the 'compare and despair' phenomenon.[3]

You probably remember how, with your own children, things began to change dramatically during late primary school. In recent years, research suggests, these changes can arrive even earlier. This is a phenomenon known as 'precocious puberty' and it is characterised by the onset of puberty at an age younger than is typical for the general population. Some countries have reported that the number of children diagnosed with precocious puberty almost doubled between 2016 and 2021, with a sharp post-2020 spike.[4]

The exact reasons for the trend are not fully understood, but are thought to involve a combination of genetic, environmental and lifestyle factors.[5] In essence, what this means is that the period of adolescence starts earlier and ends later than ever before.[6] While the physical changes of puberty may be happening earlier, many experts argue that the social and emotional changes of adolescence are taking longer to resolve, leading to a prolonged period of adolescence that extends well into the early twenties. Psychologists divide the adolescent journey into three distinct phases—early, middle and late adolescence.

Early adolescence

In this phase, your grandchild may start to seek opportunities to increase their independence and break the emotional bonds with their parents. This desire coincides with changes in the brain that increase their ability to develop more adult thought processes, such as abstract thinking. It is almost as if a neurological veil is lifted and the child begins to see adult carers in a more adult way, and to appreciate more keenly their strengths and weaknesses.

Early adolescents tend to be sensitive to any form of adult control, which can often strain their relationships with their parents—especially on family holidays. This is where grandparents can play a mediating role. Guidance is critical at this age, so grandparents should endeavour to keep the lines of communication open, even if it's mainly one way. It's all a bit of an emotional roller coaster and grandparents may not know whether to expect an eye-roll, a hug or a high-five when they meet the teenager at the front door.

Middle adolescence

Early adolescence is quickly followed by what psychologists refer to as middle adolescence. The hallmark of this period is the young person's desire for independence and autonomy, their sense of invincibility, their sexual inquisitiveness, their risk-taking urges, and their obsession with their peers.

It is in this context that middle adolescents test out their identity and use the symbols of their generation to do so: music, social media, clothes, hairstyles, and in some instances jewellery and/or piercings. At no other time in our lives is our desire to be with our age-mates so strong.

Adult carers can feel somewhat obsolete during this phase, with accompanying feelings of loss and grief.

Late adolescence

The final phase of adolescence corresponds with mid to late secondary school and sees young people pushing harder than ever for independence. This coincides with an increasing ability to be more mobile and freer of adult supervision. The emotional temperature can rise quickly.

These late-teenage years can be particularly challenging for many parents. In 2022 the Parenting Research Centre published a report called *Parenting Today in Victoria*.[7] Some 2600 parents responded to the study, which found that the parents of adolescents aged thirteen to eighteen reported feeling less effective as parents, compared to during their children's early years.

By late adolescence, most young people have come to terms with their identity and have begun to discover and define their own role in life. Their relationships with adults change, and are based much more on mutual respect and affection, as the teenagers realise that, compared to others' parents, their parents aren't so bad after all.

The good news for grandparents is that grandchildren are more responsible at this age, and some begin focusing on and even planning for the future. But they still need, and are more open to and accepting of, an adult in their life who can help them set goals and develop strategies, and whom they can use as a sounding board as they work to achieve these.

The value of experience

Up to the age of ten, grandchildren learn best by hearing, and between ten and fourteen it's by observing. But in the teenage years they learn best by experience—by doing.

As a grandparent, you can give your teenage grandchild experiences to remember. Some grandparents told me that when their grandchild turned sixteen, they offered to take them on a trip anywhere in Australia—wherever they wanted to go. Grandparent and grandchild went together and had a special one-on-one time.

Your capacity to do this will vary depending on your resources, of course, but it doesn't have to be an expensive adventure. Taking a day trip or even just learning a new activity together also offer great bonding opportunities, and can be experiences from which your grandchildren can learn life's greatest lessons.

Teenage brains

So, what do grandparents need to know about teenage grandchildren? Quite a lot, as it turns out.

Many teenagers form the view that their parents don't understand them, and they shut down communication. They want to spend more time with their friends than with their family, and this can cause conflict. They may become more preoccupied with personal image and dress, and spend more time on their appearance. One report suggests that teenagers can spend up to 7.7 hours per week in front of a mirror.[8] This can be a source of irritation to parents, but grandparents—with their greater experience—can gently suggest that parents not sweat the small stuff.

Many families report that homes with teenagers can become extremely conflictual, with much yelling, heated verbal exchanges, people storming off and doors being slammed. There is more arguing with parents, and a greater tendency to resent and resist parental authority, through testing boundaries, and

HOW DO TEENAGERS' BRAINS CHANGE?

As your grandchild matures, their brain undergoes some massive changes. Here are some of the most significant:

- The frontal cortex builds and then prunes networks throughout adolescence, which helps the brain become more efficient. This allows for a huge expansion in skills.
- In the frontal and parietal lobes, the brain similarly reinforces the most important connections. This shows up in brain scans as a noticeable increase in 'white matter'.
- As these changes happen, some brain areas develop more quickly than others, which may affect behaviour. For example, areas associated with reward tend to develop faster than those linked to self-control, which may encourage impulsive decisions.
- During adolescence, the brain becomes more responsive to dopamine, a neurotransmitter that creates good feelings, or feelings of 'reward'. Adolescents are more likely than children or adults to be drawn to novel and intense experiences.

trying to get around the rules put in place. Experimenting with sex, vaping, tobacco, alcohol or other drugs can reach a peak. Frustrations can mount as teenagers ignore parental requests and break rules, especially in relation to sleeping and waking times, and technology use.

Teenagers in this phase seek privacy, and often avoid telling parents everything that is going on. They may sometimes lie in order to do the forbidden or get themselves out of trouble. Some hate being bored and love excitement. For these teenagers, and for their parents, the astute advice of grandparents has never been more important.

Here are some tips on communicating with teenagers during this phase.

Talk less and listen more

The first rule is to talk less and listen more. The most common complaint of grandchildren is that their parents don't give them a fair hearing. When young people speak, make sure they know you're listening: put down what you're doing, turn off the TV and look at them. Listen carefully, without interrupting, and then feed back to them what they have said. This tells them not only that you have heard them, but also that you have taken their message in.

Keep it short

When you do speak, don't go on and on. This is supposed to be a dialogue, not a lecture. The average teenager has an attention span of about 13.6 seconds for what most adults have to say. So if you haven't said anything important by then, you're probably in trouble.

Use humour

Many adults use what they think is humour, but it is too often in the form of putdowns or sarcasm, which actually triggers a defensive response and shuts down the communication line they are trying to keep open. Many young people complain that their parents are too serious and need to lighten up and take a chill pill, so the appropriate use of humour is a great way to improve communication. The rules are simple: keep it upbeat and make sure that you are funny. If you're not sure, check with a friend.

Avoid issuing ultimatums

Try not to use language that triggers an adolescent's inherent sensitivity to attempts to control them. Using 'I' statements like 'I feel frustrated when I ask you to do something and you don't do it' can be a powerful communication technique when talking to teenage grandchildren because it can help to avoid blame, accusations and defensiveness, which can often trigger a shutdown in communication. Teenagers often experience a sensitivity to control because they are in a developmental stage where they are seeking more autonomy and independence, which can lead to an increased desire for control over their lives. Ultimatums are often favoured by frustrated parents; however, the risk is that the teen will take up the parents' challenge, with potentially drastic results, or the parents will have to back down and lose credibility. The trick is to think ahead. Ask yourself whether you can find a compromise solution where everyone wins a little. Grandparents can role-model this approach for the teenager's parents.

Be your grandchild's greatest fan

Regularly give your grandchild positive feedback. My teen clients often tell me that they get only one positive message for every five negative messages—many feel like they are swimming in a sea of negativity. To counter this, use descriptive praise—a form of positive reinforcement that involves describing specific behaviours or actions that the young person has done well, rather than simply giving general praise or feedback. So, instead of saying, 'Good job on that project,' descriptive praise might be: 'I really liked the way you organised your ideas and presented them clearly in your project. It shows that you put a lot of effort and thought into it.' Compliment them as often as possible on their efforts, on the strength of their character and on their individuality. Try to catch your grandchild doing something good and send them a positive message about it. Make it a goal to say at least one constructive thing each day. They may do little more than grunt, shrug and withdraw to their room. It's all about putting a deposit in the bank of goodwill for later on.

Don't constantly remind them of past mistakes

Adolescence is a time of trial and error, so mistakes are to be expected. Constantly reminding a grandchild of past stuff-ups makes it less likely they'll tell you the next time they make an error. And their lasting memory will be of a grandfather's or grandmother's monologue laced with constant criticism.

Do something together

For some grandparents, catching up over a meal or through an activity comes naturally. But one of the greatest inventions for the grandparents of teenagers is the car. When you're driving your grandchild somewhere—especially to a destination of their choice—they can't escape!

But seriously, travelling with them offers a brilliant opportunity for you to engage them in conversation—nothing too heavy, just a low-key exchange. Even finding out one important thing about your teenage grandchild's day is a great connection. It is a way of letting them know you're interested in them, their life and their point of view. You will find that teenagers are much more likely to talk if you're doing something with them.

Let some things go by you

One of the most annoying things that grandparents can do is comment on everything that an adolescent grandchild says or does. Imagine if you had someone constantly remarking on your actions throughout the day—it would be intensely irritating. Grandparents who keep up a running commentary dramatically reduce their chances of receiving any information in the future, as young people don't respond well to being constantly offered an editorial about their lives.

In summary, the teenage brain is unique in several ways. It is not very good at reading emotions, so be clear about what you mean and be patient. It is more susceptible to peer pressure, so encourage socialisation with prosocial peers—friends who behave in a way that benefits others, through sharing, caring and helping. The teenage brain is easily distracted, so remove distractions from study areas. The teenage brain struggles to get enough sleep, so teach them good sleep hygiene. It is also wired for novelty and risk, so adults need to encourage positive risk-taking.

Being the charismatic adult

Grandparenting a teenager is a balancing act. Young people crave independence and autonomy, and being a valued grandparent means finding the right combination of giving them privacy and staying connected. Although many grandkids will seek to push you away during this phase, do not allow them to reject you entirely.

There will be cases when the relationship between a teenager and their parents reaches an all-time low. This might be marked by monosyllabic or even zero communication, or by hostility, volatility, even violence. It is in these tense and emotionally turbulent situations that grandparents can play an especially valuable supportive role.

When the whole world appears to be against an agitated adolescent, it is their grandparents who can provide a listening ear and offer emotional support. Providing a non-judgemental space in which the grandchild can vent their thoughts and feelings and receive acknowledgement can make all the difference.

In my experience, there are two important life lessons all teenagers should learn. Firstly, that randomness and chaos happen in the universe—life is not always fair. And secondly, that even if you cannot change something, you can always change the way you think about it. Because of the parent–teen dynamic, the young person at various stages of the adolescent trajectory may not be able or disposed to listen to their parents. But grandparents, because their relationship with a grandchild is a bit more emotionally detached than the parent–child relationship, and usually less explosive, can gently offer a different perspective, especially as they likely have more life experience and can provide a broader view of the issues. This can help the young person gain a better understanding of the situation and make more informed decisions.

With the passage of time, and when the situation has calmed down, it is often the grandparents who can act as mediators to help both parties be heard and work towards a resolution. Grandparents can be effective advocates for a teenager's needs and wellbeing, both with their parents and in other areas of their life, such as at school or in extracurricular activities.

My experience, as a clinician working with teenagers over many years, has taught me that, more often than not, grandparents provide a stable, secure and supportive environment for the teenager during a time when some are actively resisting the gravitational pull of Planet Parent.

The adolescents with whom I work today are bombarded with information, yet they remain hungry for wisdom. They may act detached but they still need a 'charismatic adult'—indeed, they need them now more than ever. The unconditional love and acceptance teenagers usually receive from grandparents provide a natural sanctuary from the stress they may be experiencing at home or at school.

In the next chapter we consider how grandparents can best support grandchildren who face what can be challenging issues, such as coping with parental separation or divorce and loss.

The peculiar pain of separated grandparents

Hugh Mackay AO

Social psychologist and writer

When my then wife announced that she was leaving the marriage, my instinctive reaction was to say, 'What about the grandchildren?' At that stage, we had no grandchildren, but I had some painful history from a previous marriage.

The awkwardness at family gatherings: who will stand where when we pose for family photos with our arms around each other? How will we greet each other in front of the grandchildren—a peck on the cheek, a handshake, a vague smile? I recall the aching care taken over the seating arrangements at one family dinner to ensure that my ex-wife and I would be relieved of any obligation to make eye contact or conversation. That rawness eases over time, but grandchildren notice such things.

When the other grandparent turns up for the first time with a new partner, you wonder whether there will now be three people claiming grandfather status.

You need to be ready with answers to probing questions from curious minds: 'Why don't you and Grandma live together?' 'When you're married, aren't you supposed to stay married?' (Tread carefully here, or they'll be worried about the permanence of their own parents' marriage.)

Geography got in the way of close contact with most of my grandchildren, but we have become closer as they have grown up. One is married and two have just announced their engagements, and there's no awkwardness at all.

But separated prospective grandparents needn't be apprehensive: the joy of grandparenting remains unalloyed. There was a magic moment a few years ago when my youngest two grandchildren were coming over for dinner and a movie. I had *The Wizard of Oz* on hand, but my grandson seemed resistant. 'He's scared of the witch,' his sister confided to me, although it turned out he'd actually been hoping for *Saving Private Ryan*.

EIGHT

Dealing with divorce, separation and loss

According to the author Jennifer Weiner, 'Divorce isn't such a tragedy. A tragedy's staying in an unhappy marriage, teaching your children the wrong things about love. Nobody ever died of divorce.'[1] They may not die of it, but their children's separations can still cause grandparents significant heartache.

The Covid-19 pandemic created an emotional hothouse in which some families disintegrated. In a 2020 survey by Relationships Australia, 42 per cent of respondents agreed that the lockdowns and the associated isolation were negatively impacting their relationship with their partner, and as a result some elected to divorce or separate.[2] This has inevitably led to some grandparents being cut off from contact or having markedly reduced contact with their grandchildren.

Parental alienation

Following separation or divorce, there are different types of parental alienation (the psychological manipulation of a child, leading to the child rejecting or avoiding one parent without a valid reason).[3] Here are the most commonly recognised forms:

- *Mild parental alienation*: This is the least severe form. A child may be reluctant to spend time with one parent, but there is no active campaign against them by the other parent or other significant adult.
- *Moderate parental alienation*: A child may refuse to spend time with one parent and may show hostility or disrespect towards them, but there is no outright rejection.
- *Severe parental alienation*: A child may completely reject one parent and have no desire to spend any time with them. The child may also demonise the rejected parent, often using terms like 'hate', 'disgust' or 'fear' when speaking of them.
- *Parental alienation syndrome*: This refers to a situation where one parent systematically brainwashes a child to reject the other parent. The child may become obsessed with unjustified criticisms of the targeted parent, and may become unwilling or unable to have a relationship with them.

Each type of parental alienation can have varying degrees of severity, and the impact on the child and the alienated parent can also vary. It's essential to recognise and address parental alienation in order to minimise its negative effects on the child and family.

The term 'grandparent alienation' was likely coined by Dr Richard A. Warshak, a clinical psychologist and author, who highlighted the ways in which grandparents can be affected by parental alienation and can become estranged from their grandchildren as a result. Grandparent alienation can describe a situation where a child's relationship with their grandparents is negatively influenced by one or both of the child's parents, despite a prior close relationship.

In some cases, grandparent alienation can be a component of parental alienation. For example, if one parent is engaging in behaviour that is causing the child to reject the other parent, they may also be limiting contact between the child and the grandparents on the rejected parent's side. In these cases, the grandparent alienation may be a symptom of a larger pattern of family dysfunction.

The reasons for grandparent alienation can be varied and can include conflict, divorce, remarriage or a parent's manipulation of the child's thoughts and feelings towards the grandparents for any reason. Sometimes, estrangement from grandchildren can happen inadvertently: when the grandchildren relocate to a different state, territory or country, for instance, and travel is arduous or too costly. In some cases, adult carers consciously decide to separate their child from one or more grandparents.

Loss and grief

For many grandparents, family breakdown causes profound loss and grief. Grandchildren can become a hugely important part of grandparents' lives, and losing that connection creates an emotional chasm, especially when the visits stop or access dries up.

Some grandparents have described to me the anguish they feel as they walk past a room in which their grandchildren used to stay, which might still be full of toys and games. The room becomes a painful reminder of the new family circumstances; for many, it feels like they are being punished for something for which they had no responsibility.

Faced with a sudden separation, most grandparents pull out all stops to try to re-establish a connection with their grandchildren. This can be a lengthy and difficult task, and is most often negotiated through direct discussion with the in-laws, or through the legal system—which means discussions with lawyers and the Family Court.

The law and grandparents

In Australia, while grandparents do have a legal right to seek a court order permitting them to communicate with and spend time with their grandchildren, they do not enjoy automatic visitation rights, irrespective of previous childcare arrangements. In some instances, they may have to provide evidence in court that such contact would have a beneficial impact on their grandchild.

In fact, there is nothing in the *Family Law Act* that even mentions grandparents' rights to see or care for their grandchildren. The foundation of family law in Australia is that it is the young people who have rights: the court must endeavour to make decisions that are in the best interests of the child.

In an ideal world, I'd encourage, for instance, a mother to permit her children to have regular contact with her former partner's parents. The grandparents in such circumstances can play a vital role in providing predictability, love and stability for their grandchildren—especially if their parents are in the middle of an acrimonious divorce.

What predicts a successful outcome?

Divorce is stressful for all children. Research has found that kids struggle the most during the first year or two after the divorce.[4] Some kids rebound faster than others. A successful outcome is where the children get used to changes in their daily routines, grow comfortable with their living arrangements and have positive communication, parental warmth and low levels of conflict. Both parties are able to separate amicably, communicate effectively and work together to resolve issues related to the separation in a constructive and respectful manner, prioritising the wellbeing of their children and working together to create a parenting plan that is in the best interests of the children.

One predictor of a successful outcome for grandparents is the quality of thc rclationship they had with their grandchild prior to the separation. If a grandparent has been seen to be partisan or, as their child's relationship deteriorated, has been negative or unwelcoming towards their child's partner, then their relationship with the partner is likely to be acrimonious. The alienated parent may well worry that if their children are allowed to visit those grandparents, they will be brainwashed.

Alternatively, if grandparents adhere to the Grandparenting Code and have always been like the United Nations—loving and welcoming to all—then the daughter-in-law or son-in-law may have fewer reservations about permitting their child to have an ongoing relationship with the grandparents. Sadly, in my experience, when relationships break down, it is quite common for grandparents to get caught up in the psychological crossfire, irrespective of what they have said or done.

From a psychological point of view, grandparents can play a significant role in the provision of emotional support and stability to grandchildren at what is inevitably a difficult time. For children, parents' separation can be a profoundly adverse experience that undermines their identity. Research shows that a close relationship between grandparents and grandchildren can function as a protective factor against the impact.[5]

The estranged grandparent

What advice is there for the grandparent who has been cut off from this valued part of their family? Many feel powerless, especially when the circumstances dictate that there is nothing they can do. For grandparents, it is about finding ways to cope in the face of this grief.

Grief is like a fingerprint, unique to everyone, and so is the way you process it. But there are a few tried and tested things you can do to help you cope. Frankly, none of these techniques will adequately compensate for the sheer delight of spending time with a grandchild but, if executed correctly, they can at least assist you in maintaining your own wellbeing.

Talk about it

First of all, don't feel pressure to hide what you are feeling—it's better to be aware of how you feel and acknowledge it. Give sorrow words—don't bottle it up. You were involved in your grandchildren's lives and now you're not, and that's devastating. It is perfectly okay to admit you're not okay. The trick is to find someone who cares.

It's normal and healthy to feel and express intense and painful emotions when confronted with such loss. Speak to others in a similar situation. Despite how you may feel, you are not alone: sadly, grandparent alienation is common, as are the grief and anxiety that estrangement from grandchildren brings. You might connect with others on Facebook groups, for example.

If you require professional help, speak with your GP, who may refer you to a therapist or community mental health organisation or local charity. There are also online organisations such as Grandparents Australia (grandparentsaustralia.org) that specialise in supporting grandparents and advising those who have little or no contact with their grandchildren. Another route is to get in touch with Grandparents Raising Grandchildren (www.grandparentsrearinggrandchildren.org.au). These organisations can recommend a range of support services, including phone calls, video consults and web chats.

Consider a support group

You may feel tempted to ignore your feelings in this situation, but that can lead to negative side effects, including anxiety, anger or substance abuse. It's useful to acknowledge the impact estrangement has on you. A support group or therapist can help you confront and sort through your feelings.

Seek out new activities

After sharing your thoughts, and having them acknowledged and validated, consider investigating some enjoyable pastimes as you try to come to terms with the situation. Focus on what you can control. Rather than spending emotional energy on the relationship you don't have right now, find something you enjoy. Start a new interest or develop an existing one—anything that invigorates you mentally and emotionally.

Start a diary

Not only can this help you record thoughts and feelings that you may someday wish to share with your grandchildren, it can demonstrate that they were in your thoughts, despite the fact that you couldn't make contact.

Care for yourself and your partner

Estrangement can dominate your life and take a toll on your health and relationships. Remember to invest in your own and your partner's wellbeing, especially sleep, diet and exercise. And you need to be in top form, if and when the issues are resolved.

Stay neutral

A word of warning. Children hear and absorb a lot more than adults realise, and under challenging circumstances it is tempting for some grandparents to express strong feelings about the attitudes and behaviour of their grandchildren's mothers and fathers. But it is essential that your grandchildren do not hear you taking sides. Your role is to listen, stay positive and nurture.

The goal in such circumstances is, frustratingly, a long-term one, and the best mindset you can have is to be optimistic that a day will come when your grandchildren can make up their own mind about what sort of grandparent they had during these difficult times. Remaining neutral allows grandparents to plant the seeds for a bountiful future relationship. Even if physical contact is impossible, text messages, cards and presents should continue to be sent, because your grandchildren need to know that you still love them. There is, sadly, always the possibility that these may not be passed on.

Overall, grandparents can play a crucial role in helping their grandchildren navigate the challenges of parental divorce. By providing emotional support and a safe space in which children can express their feelings, and by reassuring them that they are loved and cared for, you can maintain a good relationship with them. Grandparents can offer stability, advocate for their grandchildren and mediate communication. They can also help minimise the negative impacts of a divorce on their grandchildren's mental and emotional wellbeing.

Grandparents play an important role in the lives of their grandchildren, serving as a soft spot to land during difficult times. The next chapter provides advice about how to respond when a grandchild comes to you to discuss matters of sexual orientation.

NINE

LGBTQIA+ grandchildren

It's a fact that society is evolving. Whether it's because of the many brave campaigners and advocates out there, better sex education or the legalisation of same-sex marriage, your grandchildren are part of a generation whose members feel more able than any before them to express or question their sexuality (that is, their sexual feelings, thoughts, attractions and behaviours towards other people) and/or their gender (the socially constructed characteristics of women, men, girls and boys).

Grandparents may be among the last to learn when a grandchild comes out as LGBTQIA+. It is not that the relationship is less important, however, but because the LGBTQIA+ young person might be afraid of losing that tight friendship and unconditional love which means so much to them. In this chapter I'll discuss how contemporary young people perceive gender- and sexuality-related issues and explain sexual orientation, gender expression, gender identity and how they are connected.

What does LGBTQIA+ mean?

LGBTQIA+ is an initialism that stands for lesbian, gay, bisexual, transgender, queer/questioning, intersex, asexual/aromantic and other related identities. It is an umbrella term respectfully used to refer to the diversity of individuals and capture diverse sexualities and gender identities, including (but not limited to) people who are agender, non-binary, gender fluid, asexual and pansexual, as well as individuals who prefer to use specialised personal terms to describe their own sex, gender or sexuality.

A RAINBOW GUIDE FOR GRANDPARENTS

- *Lesbian* refers to a woman who is sexually attracted to other women.

- *Gay* refers to a man who is sexually attracted to other men. It can also be used as an umbrella term for the whole LGBTQIA+ community.
- *Bisexual* refers to a person who is sexually attracted to people of their own gender and people of other genders.
- *Transgender* refers to a person whose gender identity does not match the sex that was assigned to them at birth.
- *Queer/questioning* refers to people who identify as part of the LGBTQIA+ community but may not use traditional labels.
- *Intersex* refers to individuals who are born with sex characteristics (such as chromosomes, genitals or reproductive organs) that do not fit typical male or female classifications.
- *Asexual/aromantic* refers to people who do not experience sexual or romantic attraction to others.
- The plus symbol at the end of LGBTQIA+ indicates that there are other gender and sexual identities that are not included in the initialism.

According to 2014 figures from Roy Morgan Research, the proportion of Australians who identify as LGBTQIA+ has been increasing for some time. In 2008, it was 2.4 per cent of the population, in 2011 the figure was 3.1 per cent, and by 2014 it had risen to 3.4 per cent. Today it is much higher, with 14 per cent of young Australians now identifying as gay.[1]

One thing these figures make clear is that people who consider themselves LGBTQIA+ are becoming more open about it, which we might hope reflects an increasing acceptance across society.

They also suggest there is a chance that one or more of your grandchildren may identify as LGBTQIA+, and may decide to share this aspect of their identity with you. In this chapter I discuss how best to respond.

Coming out

'Coming out' describes the process of revealing one's previously secret or just unspoken sexual orientation or gender identity to others. Typically, this means telling family members, friends or others about their LGBTQIA+ identity.

The act of coming out can be difficult and stressful for many people, as it often involves revealing a personal and potentially sensitive aspect of oneself. But coming out can also be a powerful and liberating experience for many LGBTQIA+ people, allowing them to live more authentically and connect with others with similar experiences.

It is important to note that coming out is a deeply personal decision, and should be done at a time and in a way that feels safe and comfortable for the individual. There's no right or wrong way to navigate the process. Some people may choose to come out gradually, while others may decide to make a more public announcement. The decision to come out belongs to the individual, and this should be respected by others.

Some readers might think that coming out as LGBTQIA+ is easier today than it was in times past, but my experience shows that, typically because of religious or cultural factors, it can be just as difficult, or indeed even more challenging. Despite the legalisation of same-sex marriage in Australia in 2017, and the passing of laws against discrimination on the basis of sexual orientation and gender identity, my LGBTQIA+ clients say they still face a lot of stigma and discrimination. And some other countries still criminalise homosexuality.

The experience of coming out can vary greatly, depending

on a person's individual circumstances, including their family, friends, culture and community. While progress has been made in recent years, there is still a lot of work to be done to ensure that all LGBTQIA+ individuals feel safe and supported when they decide to come out.

Disclosing one's LGBTQIA+ identity isn't always a syrupy Hollywood moment. It can happen after an incident of self-harm or a suicide attempt, or during an angry altercation, the words yelled out in frustration. Irrespective of the method of disclosure, the LGBTQIA+ person is sharing something profoundly personal, which they may have been agonising about for a long time. How you respond will be remembered, and may set a precedent for future interactions.

How should a grandparent respond?

As open-minded as you may think you are, you might still find yourself startled if your grandchild comes out to you. Over the years, many parents and grandparents have consulted me because a family member has come out. For some, this was a moral crisis, while others just wanted to know how best to help (if help was required—which is not always the case).

Your grandchild might have chosen to come out for a range of reasons. For many, hiding their true identity is stressful and exhausting. Disclosing means they can seek support and live their lives as their true selves. Coming out can be a step towards self-acceptance and self-love. Not all young people who identify as LGBTQIA+ choose to come out, but if they do, it's usually because they feel safe and ready to do so.

The most respectful first response is to stay zen. Listen, acknowledge and validate what they are saying to you about their identity. Avoid being flippant, do not interrupt and don't say anything condescending. Instead, use supportive language to assure them of your love and care—perhaps even 'I'm so glad you told me'—along with the offer of a hug. In short, your aim should be to be an ally.

Coming out can be a difficult and emotional experience for any person, and especially for an adolescent, so it is important to respond with empathy, love and support. Some young people come out to a parent first; they might not include their grandparents in the circle of trust initially. Sometimes, against the wishes of the young person, parents elect to share the news with grandparents so that they can receive support and understanding. If your grandchild comes out to you, it is important to respect their wishes regarding who you can and cannot share this information with.

WHAT IS AN ALLY?

In the context of the LGBTQIA+ community, an ally is someone who:

- supports and advocates for the rights and wellbeing of LGBTQIA+ individuals, even if they do not identify as LGBTQIA+ themselves
- acknowledges the struggles and discrimination that LGBTQIA+ people face, and actively works to create a more inclusive and accepting society
- may take many different forms of action, such as educating themselves and others about LGBTQIA+ issues, advocating for LGBTQIA+ rights and legislation, donating to LGBTQIA+ organisations, attending LGBTQIA+ events, using inclusive language, and showing support and acceptance to LGBTQIA+ friends, family members and acquaintances
- understands that discrimination against any member of the LGBTQIA+ community affects the entire community, and works towards creating a safe and welcoming environment for everyone.

The fear of family-wide rejection is very real for most young LGBTQIA+ people, so anything you can say to show your grandchild that you accept what they are telling you, and that it doesn't change your love for them, is truly the best gift you can give them. Your support can make all the difference in helping your grandchild feel safe, loved and accepted.

It may be appropriate for you to follow up by asking, 'Would you like me to do anything or talk to anyone?' Disclosing one's sexuality or gender identity isn't always a matter that needs immediate resolving—it is more likely that they just wanted you to know—but it can be absolutely draining, and they might wish to delegate you to tell someone else.

What not to say

There are many ways a grandparent can put their foot in it, but the most cringeworthy and unhelpful responses fall into three categories.

The first is the 'I knew all along' comeback. Some young people may be mortified that they either didn't conceal their secret very well or that everyone was yapping about their sexuality or gender behind their back. Your grandchild has undertaken their own unique journey to understanding themselves and their identity, and saying that you have known 'since they were a foetus' only demeans and diminishes that journey. That doesn't mean that you can't ask them about their trajectory—they may feel like sharing.

Remember, a child's sexual orientation or gender identity is an intensely private matter, and it is not helpful for you to make assumptions about your grandchild's sexual orientation based on their behaviour, interests or mannerisms. It is important to foster a safe and supportive environment in which the young person feels comfortable expressing themselves and their identity, without fear of judgement or discrimination.

The second unhelpful rejoinder is that 'this is just a phase you are going through'. This response is predicated on an assumption that being heterosexual and cisgender (that is, having a gender identity that aligns with the sex assigned at birth) is what we must aspire to, and that, in time, your grandchild will revert to 'factory settings'.

Any grandchild coming out to you is letting you know that this is who they are: this is their default setting. A dismissive response negates their emotions, creates defensiveness and dramatically reduces the potential for further conversation. Instead, be proud that you have a thoughtful and inquisitive grandchild who can open themselves up to new truths as they grow.

The last big no-no is using religion to shame them. There are some faiths that historically have opposed the idea of being LGBTQIA+ based on their interpretations of religious texts. If the young person was brought up in one of these religions, they might already be carrying some shame as a result. It's worth noting, however, that not all members of these religions hold negative beliefs about LGBTQIA+ people; indeed, there are many religious groups and leaders who advocate for LGBTQIA+ rights and acceptance.

Love and acceptance

Most of the grandparents I have met want what's best for their grandchildren, but some struggle to 'accept' their grandchild's LGBTQIA+ identity. You may not approve of the situation, but let's be honest: your approval is not required. Your love and acceptance are what is needed.

Despite social changes in recent decades, it remains a sad fact that LGBTQIA+ people have a tougher time in life. They may struggle with self-acceptance, they can be subjected to schoolyard bullying, and they often experience rejection by their families, friends and communities. Naturally enough, all this can lead to feelings of isolation and depression. LGBTQIA+ people are at higher risk of experiencing mental health issues such as anxiety and depression, and have a greater risk of suicide.

My LGBTQIA+ clients tell me that having a grandparent show up, stand up and be an active ally for them and for the broader LGBTQIA+ community has done wonders for their self-esteem and resilience. So it is well and truly over to you.

In the next chapter, we will discuss the unique challenges faced by young people who are transgender.

TEN

Transgender grandchildren

In 2018, in Hamilton County, Ohio, Judge Sylvia Sieve Hendon made legal history. She gave custody of a transgender teenager to his grandparents rather than his parents, allowing the grandparents to make medical decisions regarding his transition.[1]

According to the court report, the young person's parents had rejected their seventeen-year-old adolescent, who identified as male, refused to allow him to undergo hormone treatment and declined to call him by his chosen name, which led to him experiencing suicidal ideation. The young person had emailed a crisis hotline, claiming that 'one of his parents had told him to kill himself', and that his parents had refused to obtain counselling that was not 'Christian-based'.

The parents, for their part, had petitioned the court for custody so that they could make crucial medical decisions for the young person—specifically, they wished to stop him from obtaining the treatment suggested by his medical team.

In the landmark ruling, the judge ordered that the grandparents could apply to the court to obtain a legally binding name change for their grandchild, and that his medical costs would be covered by their health insurance. It did not endorse or validate a medical gender transition for the young person; but by allowing him to take puberty blockers, it bought him the time he needed until he turned eighteen and could legally make his own decisions.

Still, as you might imagine, the case divided the community. There were some who argued that a seventeen year-old was not capable of making such life-altering decisions. Others argued that the parents' actions were driven by 'crazy' religious beliefs and that the judge had acted in the best interests of the young person.

Across the world, legislators are trying to draft laws that give a voice to young people in situations like this. Mostly these laws aim to avoid allocating blame to the parents or involving families in protracted litigation, which can be expensive and stressful, while at the same time enabling courts to evaluate a patient's right to gender therapy.

In 2014, the Supreme Court of India issued a landmark ruling recognising transgender people as a third gender; its position was that 'recognition of transgenders as a third gender is not a social or medical issue but a human rights issue'. The court directed the Indian government to take various steps to protect the rights of transgender people and to ensure their access to education, healthcare and employment.

Since then, several measures have been taken to recognise and protect the rights of transgender people in India. For example, in 2019, the *Transgender Persons (Protection of Rights) Act* was passed, which provides for various rights and entitlements for transgender people, including the right to self-identification of gender and the right to access healthcare and education without discrimination.

What's the likelihood of your grandchild being transgender? According to researchers at the Murdoch Children's Research Institute, about 1.2 per cent of children in Australia are thought to identify as transgender—which is approximately 45,000 children.[2] The number of referrals to the Royal Children's Hospital Gender Service has grown considerably in recent years, with 473 new referrals in 2020.[3]

Some definitions

So what is it that grandparents need to know about such cases? Well, it begins with the term 'gender', which turns out to be more complex than most of us were taught when we were young. Indeed, if you were brought up in the 1950s, modern notions of gender might be difficult to comprehend. We live in a world where gender identity is increasingly considered a cultural construct and a fluid concept. Before rushing to judgement about that, it is important that grandparents become familiar with the conversation.

A 'transgender' grandchild generally refers to a child who was assigned as male at birth but identifies as female, or a child who was assigned female but identifies as male.

'Cisgender', as we saw in the previous chapter, describes someone whose gender identity aligns with the sex they were assigned at birth. A cisgender grandchild is one who identifies as male or female and was assigned that same gender at birth, based on their biological sex.

A 'gender-diverse' grandchild refers to one who may have an assortment of gender identities and practices, who may combine different genders, or who may identify as having a non-binary gender.

'Non-binary' refers to someone who may not be exclusively male or female. They may use pronouns to signal their non-binary gender, such as 'they/them'. Individuals who identify as non-binary may see themselves as falling outside of the traditional gender binary of male and female, or they may see themselves as a mix of both, or somewhere in between.

'Gender identity' and 'sexual orientation' are two different things. Being transgender is about an individual's gender identity—that is, whether they feel male, female, a little of both or neither. Being gay, lesbian or bisexual is about an individual's sexual orientation, which is our sexual or romantic attraction to people of the same gender, a different gender, both or neither. While many children who go on to identify as lesbian, gay or bisexual express gender-expansive behaviours, whether they are transgender is about their identity rather than who they are attracted to.

Everyone possesses both a gender identity and a sexual orientation. For instance, a transgender person can also identify as gay, lesbian or bisexual.

Is this new?

Many grandparents wonder whether the modern understanding of gender and identity is a new phenomenon. Given that the span of recorded human history is approximately 5000 years, it's noteworthy that many flourishing cultures during that time have not only recognised but sometimes revered more than two genders.[4]

CULTURES THAT HAVE RECOGNISED MORE THAN TWO GENDERS

- *Native American Two-Spirit People*: Many indigenous North American cultures have a traditional third or fourth gender category, often referred to as 'two-spirit'. Two-spirit people are often seen as having both male and female spirits, and are considered important members of their communities.
- *Hijra in India*: Hijra are individuals in India who are assigned male at birth but identify as feminine or non-binary. Hijra have a long history in India, and have been recognised as a distinct gender category for centuries.

- *Fa'afafine in Samoa*: Fa'afafine are individuals in Samoa who are assigned male at birth but identify and live as feminine or non-binary. Fa'afafine are widely accepted in Samoan culture and play important roles in their communities.
- *Sworn virgins in Albania*: Sworn virgins are individuals in Albania who are assigned female at birth but take on masculine roles and identities, often so they can inherit property or carry on family traditions.
- *Kathoey in Thailand*: Kathoey are individuals in Thailand who are assigned male at birth but identify as feminine or non-binary. Kathoey are recognised as a distinct gender category in Thai society, and are often visible in the entertainment industry.

Despite the fact that transgender people have been present in society for millennia, in Australia respectful discussion about gender has increased at a snail's pace over the past two decades. Many people still hold the belief that being transgender or gender-diverse (also referred to as 'trans') is a mental health problem, rather than part of the natural spectrum of human diversity.

Some young trans people do experience a condition known as gender dysphoria, as well as other mental health concerns. Gender dysphoria is the often significant distress felt by people whose gender (that is, their sense of being male, female or something else) differs from the gender assigned to them at birth based on their genital appearance.

This condition can be treated in a variety of ways, including counselling, hormone therapy and gender-affirming surgeries. These treatments are aimed at reducing distress and improving quality of life for individuals with gender dysphoria. It is important to approach gender dysphoria with sensitivity and respect, and to avoid stigmatising or pathologising individuals based on their gender identity.

The challenges faced by transgender people

The distress that can accompany gender dysphoria is not just caused by the individual's identity, but also by the social and cultural constraints and stigma associated with not conforming to traditional gender roles. The transgender or gender-diverse clients that I have seen over the years experience three main challenges.

Mental health challenges

Children who are transgender or gender-diverse may experience mental health challenges due to discrimination, and the ways in which they are treated and positioned in society. Transgender or gender-diverse people have higher rates of anxiety, depression, self-harm and/or attempted suicide than the general population. Some 82 per cent of transgender individuals have considered killing themselves, and 40 per cent have attempted suicide, with suicidality highest among transgender youth.[5]

Negative school experiences

Children spend a lot of their time in school. While some transgender and gender-diverse children have positive experiences at school, this is often not the case. Negative school experiences include difficulties with peers and friendships, harassment and violence, fears for safety, social exclusion, and issues in relation to uniforms, toilets and sports. Children may miss school or change schools to avoid such negative experiences, resulting in a disrupted routine, with potentially long-term consequences for their mental health, educational achievement and future employment prospects.

Fear of puberty

The physical changes of puberty—such as developing breasts, growing body and facial hair, and a deepening voice—can be particularly distressing for transgender and gender-diverse children.

A 2020 study of 300 transgender young people found that mental distress—including self-harm, suicidal thoughts and depression—amplified as the children were forced to proceed with puberty according to their assigned sex.[6] By the time 184 older teens (with a median age of sixteen) reached the stage in which transgender boys began their periods and grew breasts, and transgender girls' voices dropped and facial hair began to appear, 46 per cent had been diagnosed with depression, 40 per cent had self-harmed, 52 per cent had considered suicide and 17 per cent had attempted it—rates significantly higher than those of younger transgender children and of cisgender kids their own age.

How might a transgender grandchild express their identity?

It is important to recognise that our gender identity is a deeply personal and complex aspect of our identity, and that every child's experience is unique. Only the child themselves can truly know and express their gender identity.

At some point, nearly all grandchildren will engage in behaviour typically associated with different genders—girls will play with trucks, boys will play with dolls, girls will hate wearing dresses and boys will insist on wearing them. Behaviour like this ('gender nonconforming behaviour') does not necessarily mean that a child is transgender. That said, sometimes these behaviours can help us understand what a child is feeling about their gender. Some children identify as belonging to a gender other than the one they were assigned at birth by the time they are toddlers.

There are nevertheless some signs that a grandchild might be transgender. These can include the following:

- Persistent and consistent statements that they are not the gender they were assigned at birth. For example, a child who was assigned male at birth but who consistently says they are a girl.
- Strong feelings of discomfort or distress with their body or with the gender roles and expectations placed upon them by society. For example, a child assigned female at birth who is consistently uncomfortable with wearing dresses or being referred to as 'she'.

- Behaviours or preferences that are more commonly associated with the gender they identify as. For example, a child assigned female at birth who consistently prefers playing with traditionally masculine toys and participating in typically masculine activities.

It's noteworthy that children who display these signs will not necessarily be transgender—and that every child's experience is unique. It is important to create a safe and supportive environment in which the child feels comfortable expressing themselves and their gender identity, and to seek the guidance of qualified professionals, such as a therapist or paediatrician who specialises in gender-identity issues.

The role of grandparents

As the Ohio court ruling shows, grandparents can play an important role in the lives of their transgender grandchildren. Here are some things to keep in mind:

- Acceptance and support from all family members is crucial. Transgender children need the love and support of their family, including their grandparents. Showing support and love for your grandchild can have a huge and positive impact on their mental health and wellbeing.

- If your grandchild has chosen a new name or pronouns, making an effort to use them will show the child that you respect and accept their gender identity. Not doing so is a violation of the Grandparenting Code.
- It's okay to ask questions and learn. Naturally you will have questions or concerns when a grandchild comes out as transgender, and it's important to approach the topic with an open mind and a willingness to learn. Ask your grandchild what you can do to support them, and seek out resources to help you understand what they are going through.[7]

What not to do

- Don't make any assumptions about how your grandchild would like to be referred to. Ask them.
- Don't ask about what genitals your grandchild has or will have, especially as a factor in deciding how you'll refer to them.
- Don't explain away your grandchild's preference based on how it affects you.

- Don't use your grandchild's previous name. This is called 'deadnaming', and it's disrespectful. If you're unsure how to refer to them in the past, ask them.
- Don't out them. If you happen to learn about your grandchild's preference or that they may be having treatment, keep it to yourself.

Facing the future

For some transgender children, medical treatment known as 'gender-affirming care' can be important. Medical interventions such as puberty blockers or hormone therapy may be necessary to alleviate gender dysphoria. Some transgender people may choose to pursue sex reassignment surgery. Medical transitioning is a highly personal choice, and it is offensive to ask someone if they have done so or will do so. Your grandchild's transition may also include social transitioning and legal transitioning.

If your grandchild is considering medical treatment, it's important for you to listen to their needs and help them access professional medical and psychological support.

Overall, the most important thing for grandparents to remember is that their transgender grandchild is the same person they have always been, and they need the love and support of their family now more than ever. Research suggests that the situation for transgender children will only improve if we reduce societal discrimination and ensure the availability of safe, low-cost and accessible mental health support services, as well as gender-affirming medical and surgical interventions for those who need them.

A supportive community of grandparents can facilitate an inclusive Australia that embraces diversity and supports all people, including our most vulnerable, to have a 'fair go'; receive quality, evidence-based healthcare; work, study and live safely; and reach their full potential.

ELEVEN
Neurodiverse grandchildren

For most grandparents, nothing can compare with the boundless love they feel for their grandchildren. No longer under pressure to balance work, home, school and raising their own children, many see grandchildren as one of life's greatest blessings.

But life doesn't always deliver its gifts in the package we expect. Some grandchildren will be identified as 'neurodiverse'. This refers to the concept that there is natural variation in human neurocognitive functioning, and that this diversity should be recognised and respected. In other words, not everyone's brain is wired the same—and that is okay.

The neurodiversity movement is a social justice movement that seeks to change the way society views and treats individuals with neurological differences. Its members maintain that this diversity should be celebrated and valued, rather than stigmatised or pathologised. The movement emerged in the 1990s, led largely by individuals on the autism spectrum, but it has since expanded to include a range of other conditions that typically affect communication, social interaction and behaviour.

The label 'neurodiverse' can encompass a range of conditions, including:

- autism spectrum disorder (ASD)
- attention deficit hyperactivity disorder (ADHD)
- dyslexia and other specific learning difficulties
- Tourette syndrome and other tic disorders
- dyspraxia (developmental coordination disorder)
- synaesthesia
- giftedness and high IQ
- sensory processing disorder (SPD)
- nonverbal learning disorder (NVLD)
- bipolar disorder
- schizophrenia
- obsessive-compulsive disorder (OCD)
- anxiety disorders
- depression.

It's important to note that not everyone who has one of these conditions will identify as neurodiverse, and some who do not have a formal diagnosis may still identify as neurodiverse.

You may also have heard the term 'Asperger's syndrome'.[1] In the past this was considered a separate diagnosis from autism, but it is now considered a subtype of autism spectrum disorder (ASD). Individuals who would previously have been diagnosed with Asperger's syndrome are now diagnosed with ASD.

The main difference between what was known as Asperger's syndrome and other types of autism is the absence of a significant delay in language development or cognitive functioning in children with Asperger's syndrome. However, they still have difficulties with social interactions, communication, and restricted or repetitive behaviours, similar to individuals with other types of autism.

In this chapter, we will discuss the unique series of challenges facing grandparents whose grandchild has one of the more common diagnoses, autism spectrum disorder. Grandparents seeking advice on how they might help grandchildren with other forms of neurodiversity should talk with the child's parents, offer to accompany them to the paediatrician or psychologist, and become as educated as possible.

Autism spectrum disorder

If your grandchild has been diagnosed as being on the autism spectrum, it means their brain is wired differently. ASD is called a 'spectrum' disorder because the symptoms and severity can vary widely among individuals. Autism is typically diagnosed in early childhood, and the exact cause is not yet fully understood. However, it is believed to be the result of a combination of genetic and environmental factors.

ASD affects one in every 100 to 110 individuals in Australia. It is a lifelong condition, meaning your grandchild will not 'grow out of it', and there is no cure. Autistic people can also be diagnosed with ADHD, dyspraxia (motor-system difficulties), dyslexia (reading difficulties), epilepsy, anxiety disorders and many other conditions.

A helpful way of understanding this condition, as autism expert Professor Tony Attwood puts it, is that ASD children have found something more interesting in life than socialising. Many people with ASD struggle to understand social cues, to make eye contact and to engage in reciprocal conversation. Their heightened or reduced sensitivity to certain sensory stimuli, such as touch, sound or smell, can make social situations overwhelming or uncomfortable, leading to avoidance and isolation.

You might notice that ASD grandchildren make fewer gestures than typical children, understand fewer phrases (language delay) and find certain objects fascinating, becoming fixated on the colour symmetry and patterns they see. Some may show an interest in visually repetitive phenomena, such as spinning objects, and can find comfort in the predictability and consistency of visual repetition.

Please remember that these signs of autism are just a general guide—not all children with autism will exhibit all these behaviours.

ASD is generally diagnosed more frequently in children than in adults. According to the Australian Government's Institute of Health and Welfare, 83 per cent of Australians with autism are under 25, with a diagnosis being most common among children aged between five and fourteen.[2]

A diagnosis of ASD is, for some families, a psychological bolt from the blue. Many people have never heard of the condition, or have only vague knowledge of it, often associated with fictional characters such as Dr Sheldon Cooper from *The Big Bang Theory*.

The response of family members to a diagnosis of ASD can vary widely, depending on the child's circumstances and the parents' experiences, beliefs and values. Some feel shock and disbelief, others loss and sadness, as they come to terms with the fact that their child may face challenges that other children will not. Some families feel guilt and self-blame, questioning whether they could have done something differently to prevent their child from having ASD.

If you have an autistic grandchild, your first task is to get informed. There are many excellent websites where you can read about ASD, including raisingchildren.net.au. The signs of autism can appear in early childhood, and it's important to recognise them as early as possible so that intervention can be provided.

Pathological demand avoidance (PDA)

As a grandparent of a child on the spectrum, you may read about or be told of something called pathological demand avoidance (PDA).[3] PDA was first named by the late British psychologist Elizabeth Newson in the 1980s. Newson was a pioneering figure in the field of autism research, and her work on PDA was based on her observations of a small group of children who exhibited a distinct profile of behaviour that was different from that

MOVIES THAT FEATURE CHARACTERS WITH ASD

- *Rain Man* (1988): This classic film stars Dustin Hoffman as Raymond, an autistic savant who is taken on a road trip by his younger brother, played by Tom Cruise. The film won several Academy Awards, including Best Picture.
- *Mercury Rising* (1998): In this action thriller, Bruce Willis plays an FBI agent who must protect a young autistic boy who has cracked a top-secret government code.
- *Temple Grandin* (2010): This biopic tells the true story of a woman with autism who revolutionised the livestock industry with her designs for humane animal-handling facilities. The film stars Claire Danes as Grandin and won several Emmy Awards.
- *Extremely Loud & Incredibly Close* (2011): This drama follows a young boy named Oskar (played by Thomas Horn) as he searches for a lock that fits a key left behind by his father, who died in the September 11 attacks. Oskar is portrayed as having some autistic traits, although he is not explicitly diagnosed in the film.

- *The Accountant* (2016): In this action thriller, Ben Affleck plays an autistic accountant who is also a skilled assassin. The film received mixed reviews but was a commercial success.

of other children on the autism spectrum. It is important for grandparents to know about PDA because the behaviour can put a significant strain on relationships within the family and with friends.

PDA describes a profile of ASD where children exhibit high levels of anxiety and a need for control, which manifests in a resistance to everyday demands and expectations.

While many children experiment with rebellion and resisting parental authority, what sets PDA apart is that it can lead to a persistent and pervasive resistance even to demands that seem routine or minor. Children with PDA may use avoidance strategies, such as distraction or negotiation, to maintain a sense of control. They may also display behaviours that appear manipulative or oppositional, such as lying, avoidance or even aggression, in order to resist demands.

Notice your grandchild's behaviours

In 30 per cent of cases, it is the grandparents—perhaps because of their greater experience of childrearing—who are the first to suspect that there is something amiss with their grandchild's development.[4] One grandparent I spoke to told me that she suspected ASD when she noticed that her grandchild did not respond to their name. Some grandparents pick up on the fact that their grandchild may have a limited range of facial expressions,[5] walk around on tiptoes,[6] tend not to smile or look at other people,[7] and have unusual hand and finger mannerisms.[8]

Avoiding interaction

Many autistic children are not very good at understanding people, which is why they tend not to make eye contact[9] or engage others in back-and-forth play[10] or conversation. You may also notice that your grandchild is not interested in social games or turn-taking. They may show a preference for being alone, and may be quite content in that solitude, even resisting attempts by others to engage with them.[11]

Repetitive behaviours

Your ASD grandchild may engage in repetitive behaviours,[12] such as hand flapping, rocking back and forth or lining up their toys. Some may have narrow and intense interests (trains, dinosaurs) that they talk about frequently.[13] They may have difficulty transitioning from one activity to another, or may become upset when there are changes to their routine. Variety is not the spice of life with ASD kids—most tend not to like surprises.

Sensory play

Children with autism may not engage in imaginative play, such as pretending to be a superhero or having a tea party with their stuffed toys. They can be more interested in exploring the world via their senses. Exploring the world's sensory qualities can help autistic children regulate their emotions and behaviour. Sensory bins are containers which include materials like sand, rice, beans and water, and children are encouraged to touch, explore and manipulate materials using their hands or tools such as spoons or scoops. They provide a hands-on, immersive play opportunity for children, being filled with materials and objects that stimulate the senses. They can also help children overcome aversions to different textures in a safe environment.

Sensory sensitivities

Sensory sensitivities are common among individuals with autism, and your grandchild with ASD may exhibit acute sensitivity to sounds such as other kids shouting, hairdryers, vacuum cleaners, barking dogs or teachers who yell.[14] They may be hypersensitive to smells and find certain odours, such as perfume, overwhelming or unpleasant.[15] Some may refuse to eat certain foods,[16] and may be unable to tolerate being in public places like malls or restaurants.

Food

Because autistic children can be hypersensitive to certain textures, tastes or smells, eating can be difficult or even painful. Some children may have a restricted range of foods they are willing to eat, which can lead to nutritional deficiencies and challenges in social situations where only limited food options are available. Some children may need to eat the same food every day, or may refuse to eat anything that is not a certain colour or texture.

Panic

Autistic children may experience panic or anxiety in a variety of situations. This panic response can be triggered by overwhelming sensory inputs, such as loud noises, bright lights or crowded spaces, or if their routine is disrupted—because of a change in schedule, for example. Typically, ASD children cannot be consoled by affection or distraction; adult carers simply have to wait until the storm passes.

Strategies for grandparenting children with ASD

Grandparents may be anxious about doing the wrong thing as they try to forge connections with their ASD grandchild. While every child with ASD is unique, there are some general principles that you may find helpful.

All children with ASD will have their individual strengths and weaknesses. They may do some things very well, and struggle with others. Regardless, they need your love and respect. Always keep in mind, however, that they may not react well to tried-and-true parenting techniques. What may seem like 'bad' behaviour could actually be a reaction to feeling overwhelmed and stressed, or perhaps extremely frustrated. Here are some tips to help you help them.

Identify their specific triggers

It's important to work out what causes your grandchild to feel anxiety, and to develop strategies to address these triggers. These may include providing sensory tools to help them regulate their emotions; creating and sticking to a predictable routine; or using visual aids to help them understand and prepare for unfamiliar situations. Working with a qualified therapist or counsellor can also be beneficial in helping the child develop coping strategies and build resilience to manage their panic or anxiety. Involving the child in the development of their coping strategies can help them feel empowered and more in control of their emotions.

Learn about your ASD grandchild's preferences and sensitivities

Each child with ASD will have their own unique preferences and sensitivities. Some autistic children will enjoy cuddles, for instance, while others may not. It's important to respect the individual needs and preferences of each child, and to communicate with them in a way that is comfortable and respectful.

There is nothing wrong with asking your grandchild if they are okay with physical contact before initiating a cuddle.

Find out what they like

Like most children, your grandchild with ASD needs to have fun! Find out what they like—puzzles, cars, Barbie movies?—and use these activities to spend quality time with them. Focus on your grandchild, not on their autism. If your grandchild likes to play alone or alongside you (rather than directly with you), that's okay. Always remember that they may struggle with interpreting body language, facial expressions, tones of voice, jokes, satire and emotional situations, so you may need to take extra care when talking with them.

Speak normally

Even if your grandchild is shouting, maintain a normal speaking voice. Anyone yelling will raise the emotional temperature, especially if the child is sensitive to loud noises. So make sure that everyone uses their inside voice. Loud noises can cause sensory overload, leading to increased anxiety, stress and even physical pain or discomfort.

Create a safe place for them to go when stressed

Construct a peaceful, protected sanctuary for your ASD grandchild within your home, somewhere they can go if they're feeling stressed or overwhelmed. Ensure they have a much-loved object that is a source of comfort to them. If you pick up your grandchild after school, they'll be exhausted and will benefit from having a place to retreat to and unwind. Let them watch TV, spend time in their quiet place or do anything else they find calming.

Use diagrams

Create a pictorial schedule of prearranged events that your grandchild might do with you and place it on the wall or fridge. Checking off events as they are completed creates a sense of order, predictability and routine for them.

A broad spectrum

While around 1 in 100 children are diagnosed with autism, up to 30 per cent of people may have at least one of the traits associated with the disorder. Autism is known as a 'spectrum' disorder because there is a wide variation in the type and severity of symptoms people experience. Low-functioning autism (LFA) is a degree of autism marked by difficulties with social communication and interaction, challenging behaviour, and differences in social or emotional reciprocity. Some children may suffer sleep problems, aggression, stereotypical behaviour (semi-voluntary repetitive movements), and self-injurious behaviour, all of which can negatively impact on parent and family functioning and create significant stress.

Irrespective of where their grandchild is on the spectrum, grandparents can help their autistic grandchildren be themselves. These children see the world through different eyes: they often notice details and patterns that other people miss. This can lead to great originality in problem-solving, which is why some of the world's greatest inventions have been made by people who have autism.[17] They often have a unique perspective on the world, challenging conventional ways of thinking, and promoting diversity and inclusivity, which can lead to fresh insights. The world needs your grandchild with autism.

Reflections of a type A grandfather

Gordon Parker AO

Scientia Professor of Psychiatry, University of NSW, founder of the Black Dog Institute

Credentials: eleven grandchildren, covering four of Shakespeare's seven ages of man, from infant through to gainfully employed.

No rocking chair for me! I am a driven, impatient, type A personality who needs to be busy and has firmly resisted retirement: you can predict my profile as a grandfather. I've also resisted fond monikers such as 'Granddad' or 'Pop' (I just don't feel 'that old'), while my wife readily welcomed the title of 'Nanna'. This explains why one grandchild once referred to us as 'Nanna and her very best friend who lives with her'.

I observe my wife and so many friends who are in 'flow' with their grandchildren, spending pleasurable amounts of time playing and reading with them or just sitting next to them as they watch *Bluey*, content and fulfilled. I regret that I have never been able to realise such a rhythm—leopards and spots are in play.

But there have been, and continue to be, great pleasures in my role as titular observer. Initially, in observing our own children—their once feckless adolescent personalities transmuting into wonderfully caring and responsible parents. I didn't see that coming; I must have missed that lecture during psychiatry training. Later, my pleasure has stemmed from observing our grandchildren's diversity—some academic, some sporty and some artistic. And their imagination at family get-togethers, organising concerts and other entertainments—when not preoccupied with their mobile phones. (Ahh! Here I have to activate *my* mute button.) And the years following—when they bring their partners to family get-togethers. Circle of life stuff—and relished.

But I can blunder at such times. Once, in a Christmas quiz I'd organised for them, I included the question 'Who is the most modest grandchild?'. I anticipated the fun: viz., all but one yelling, 'ME, ME, ME, ME!' The problem was that I provided my answer. The group hurt was palpable.

Probably best if I remain an observer.

TWELVE

Preserving your family's history

Grandparents are a living link between a family's past and its future. Their intimate knowledge about the two generations that preceded them and the two that follow gives them insight into the lives of five generations. Passing on that knowledge is important for preserving both family heritage and cultural identity.

As someone who never met his grandparents on either side of the family, I am acutely aware of how scant my knowledge of my ancestors is. My family tree is more like a bonsai than a great oak. The Grandparenting Code stipulates that a significant task for grandparents is to pass on stories and information that will help their children and grandchildren learn more about their heritage.

I have managed to secure a few tantalising details from genealogical research, my memories of chats with my parents (both now deceased) and one memorable visit to a tiny village in Lincolnshire, where my grandfather was the local vicar for many years. I even met people who had known my grandfather on my mother's side. I definitely have more genealogical research to do and site visits to make.

For some reason, I never had much interest in history at school, but as I grew older I found it more interesting to learn from those who had lived it. I learned about the Blitz, for instance, because my father had been in London at the time and served in the RAF. For me, personal stories are more engaging and easier to remember than lists of names and dates.

The family historian

As a grandparent, you are the custodian of what your family has experienced and endured over the years. You are the keeper of your family history, and your grandchildren will benefit enormously from learning about it. If you can pass those memories on, you will help them develop a sense of belonging and security. Apart from being a source of unconditional love and acceptance, of all the contributions grandparents can make to their grandchildren, few are more important than giving them a sense of how they fit into the history of their family.

Family storytelling is more than just a superb bonding mechanism. Researchers at Emory University in Atlanta, Georgia, asked 48 families twenty questions about their family history. They found that the more the children knew, the stronger their sense of control over their lives, the higher their self-esteem and the more successfully they felt their families functioned. Hearing these stories gave the children a sense of their history and a strong 'intergenerational self'. The bottom line was that children who had a strong 'family narrative' enjoyed better emotional health.[1]

How can grandparents help pass on family history?

The mnemonic to help you remember this is PPTS, which stands for Places, Photos, Tree and Stories.

Places: revisit significant locations

Grandparents can connect their grandchild with the past, pass on family memories and make memories with them in the present by visiting places of great significance to the family. This might be the house, suburb, town or city in which the grandparents grew up. Walking a grandchild through the old family home, driving them around the old neighbourhood and sharing memories of who lived next door or down the road is psychological gold. Discussing the people you were close to with them makes the memories come alive. Taking a video or photo as you do so will ensure that the trip and memories will be preserved for them to revisit in the future.

Photos: curate images of your family members

Create a 'photo wall'. Whether you collect images in one large frame or in a series of frames, the Grandparenting Code suggests that you create a special area in your home reserved for your family photos. When your grandchildren visit, you can, over time, explain who is who, perhaps mentioning what occupation they had, what sort of person they were and what made them unique. The photo wall could be augmented by a family photo album, either online or in printed form. I'm sure you will find that going through old photographs with your grandchildren is an enjoyable way to share family history.

Tree: research your family history

If you don't already have a family tree, search through your possessions to locate photos, documents and personal correspondence that might help you create one. Items with dates are especially helpful. Family memorabilia might include old pictures, military records, diplomas and report cards, and—of course—diaries, postcards and letters. Several free and fee-based online genealogical databases might also be helpful, including Ancestry, the world's largest online family history resource. The payoff for all this detective work is that you can time-travel through your family history with your grandchildren beside you. Not only will you get to know your ancestors in a more intimate and meaningful way, you'll also be giving your grandchildren a tangible link to their cultural heritage and family history.

Stories: share your memories

Oral traditions are an important part of many cultures and can serve multiple purposes: preserving history, sharing values and beliefs, and fostering a sense of community and identity. The power of stories lies in their ability to teach, inspire, entertain, preserve and heal. Stories have the ability to connect generations by sharing experiences, traditions and emotions. They can create a sense of intergenerational empathy and understanding. Well-told stories can also be highly entertaining, especially when the teller uses humour, drama or suspense.

A recent survey by the American Association of Retired Persons found that grandparents often see their role as passing on strong values, with 78 per cent acknowledging that they have discussed morals and values with their grandkids.[2] Many of my young clients, I have discovered over the years, have an almost unlimited desire to learn about the 'olden days', and storytelling is a wonderful way for grandparents to teach their life lessons.

Grandfriends Day

Some schools hold an event called Grandparents Day, which is often renamed as Grandfriends Day—a move that has attracted some criticism.[3] Schools justified the name change by arguing that they had invited residents from a local aged-care facility who were penpals with the students, and that the name change provided an opportunity for students who might have lost their

CREATING YOUR OWN ORAL HISTORY RECORD

If you have memories that you would like to record for posterity, one of the best ways to do so is by creating an oral history. Here are some tips to help you go about it.

- Write down an initial list of stories or memories that you would like to capture.
- Decide on a time and place for the audio or video storytelling to occur. If possible, ask a grandchild to assist you. You may find it easier to respond to questions from a family member, rather than facing the camera alone.
- Prepare and practise with your audio or video capture technology—a video camera, smartphone, tablet or similar technology—and test it before you begin.
- Conduct a series of short recording sessions to capture and record the memories you want to preserve. Share the audio or video files with your grandchildren and other family members, and make sure to save the files in an organised way on a computer.

grandparents to feel included in the day's celebrations. I would welcome a move to make it 'Grandparents and Grandfriends Day', because my sense is that the decision to remove grandparents from the title is counterproductive.

Whatever you call it, the day allows grandparents (and others) to visit classrooms and see their grandkids in their educational environment and share their legacy. Grandparents have the ability to take a class of students on a journey back through time—to an era that young people of today's generation can only read about in books or see in footage on YouTube.

Celebrate your family's heritage

Grandparents can play an important role in helping their grandchildren celebrate diversity within their family and develop a sense of pride in their cultural background. You can share stories and traditions from your culture, including recipes and customs. If it's practical, you can take your grandchildren to visit cultural landmarks and museums that celebrate different cultures. This can be a fun and educational experience, but will also help them develop an appreciation for diversity. Children can also learn about their heritage by attending cultural events, such as festivals and concerts, and by being exposed to different foods, music and art.

If grandchildren come from a bilingual or multilingual family, grandparents can encourage them to learn the language(s) of their heritage. Bilingual children have been shown to have improved cognitive development, including better problem-solving skills, improved academic performance, increased creativity and better critical-thinking abilities.[4] Having another language can also open up more job opportunities for children in the future, in fields such as business, diplomacy and translation.

Keep a grandchild record

At the end of this book is an example of a grandchild record, which grandparents can use to document their grandchild's growth and development, milestones and special moments. This record can be passed down through generations and serve as a family keepsake. Additionally, the record can help grandparents stay involved in their grandchild's life, even if they live far away. It can also help grandparents remember important details about their grandchild's life and serve as a tool for reminiscing and storytelling. Finally, keeping a grandchild record can help grandparents feel a sense of purpose and fulfilment in their role as their families continue to grow.

Share the responsibility

As we have seen, grandparents play a vital role in preserving and passing on family history, but they are not the sole custodians of it. Family history is the responsibility of all members of a family, and can be passed down from generation to generation through a variety of means, including oral traditions, written records, photographs and other artefacts.

While grandparents have a wealth of personal experiences and memories to share, it is also important for younger generations to take an active interest in their family history, and to seek out information and materials that can help preserve it. This can involve asking questions, conducting research, and collecting and organising the family records and artefacts.

In the end, the preservation and transmission of family history requires the participation and cooperation of all family members. But in my view, the initial spark should come from the older generation. By working together, families can ensure that their history is passed down to future generations and will remain a source of pride and connection for years to come.

Being a great *grandparent*

Eric Tweedale ASM
Wallabies prop, 1946–49

Being now 102, I can look back on a very long life and say it's all about learning—including learning to be a great-grandparent.

Before World War II, I played first-grade cricket as a pace bowler for Cumberland with Richie Benaud's father, Lou—he used to bring Richie to practise against us senior players (now that's good parenting!). Not long after the war broke out, I joined the navy as a signalman, and after the war I played ten Tests for the Wallabies and dozens of tour matches in New Zealand, Britain, Ireland, France and the United States. I also played rugby for New South Wales and had a long club career at Parramatta. One thing I've learned, however, is that nothing in sport—or war—can prepare you for being a parent, a grandparent or a great-grandparent.

In my day, we didn't think of parenting or grandparenting as a 'thing'—you just did it. I became a parent in 1946 and have three grandchildren and six great-grandchildren, who've all been active and sporty. My first grandchildren, twin girls, were born in 1969, and my most recent great-grandchild arrived in 2014.

The best thing about being a great-grandparent? I think it's seeing the results of the little bit of work you did. When you get to a great age, you can't interact with them that much, but they love going for rides on the walker!

Do I find anything about it challenging? Well, it's much easier than parenting, but you do need to be patient. I've always been a kids man—I used to coach 70 juniors at Parramatta after my playing days had finished—so having grandkids and great-grandkids has brought me a great deal of happiness.

I'm proud to say that I've learned a lot about parenting—and grandparenting—from my daughter and son-in-law. It goes to show that learning is not a one-way process.

THIRTEEN

Grandparenting superglue

This book has introduced you to the Grandparenting Code. As well as common sense, and a good dollop of the bleeding obvious, it is based on solid psychological theories developed over many years.

Some grandparents I chatted to for the book asked me what the research said was the age at which their grandchildren might drift away from them. The answer, of course, as it is so often in psychology, is that it depends. The circumstances vary: upbringing, geography, personality traits and lifestyle factors all play a role. What happens varies quite a bit from family to family.

In general terms, my experience is that teenagers seek independence and autonomy, and often their friends become the number one priority. So, when grandchildren reach around ten years of age, unless grandparents make a special effort, contact can lessen.

The good news is that there are evidence-based strategies that can help keep the relationship going. Research has also found some clear patterns that help to determine why some grandparents are closer to their grandchildren than others.

It makes sense that how the members of each generation relate to one another is a major component of grandparenting, and social psychologists Merril Silverstein and Vern L. Bengtson have created a model known as 'intergenerational solidarity' to investigate grandparenting practices across the lifespan and in different cultures.[1]

There are six key ingredients that create this 'solidarity', or relationship closeness, which in turn creates the grandparenting magic we have been discussing. Because they are academics, they have used some pretty fancy language to explain the pieces of the theory—the types of solidarity they identified are structural, associational, consensual, affectual, functional and normative solidarity.

Despite the jargon, I think that if you can wrap your head around these concepts and embrace even some of them, the odds are stratospherically high that you will have the psychological skills to ensure a lasting relationship with your grandchild.

So, bear with me as we demystify these ideas and learn about what I like to call grandparenting superglue.

Structural solidarity

The first part of Silverstein and Bengtson's model is what they refer to as 'structural solidarity'. They talk about how important it is to have the 'opportunity structure for cross-generational interaction to reflect geographic proximity between family members'. What this means in everyday English is that living near your grandchildren is one of the strongest predictors of having a close relationship with them.

Duh! Obviously, it is easier to give and get material help, care and support if family members live in the same suburb, city or state. Even if you don't live next door, being physically close beats the hell out of living across the world. As we saw in Chapter 4, this impact is partially mitigated by modern technologies, such as Skype, Zoom and WhatsApp, which all facilitate communication between family members who are distant from one another.

Associational solidarity

Silverstein and Bengtson next talk about 'associational solidarity'. Just living nearby is not enough to create a close bond, they say; you also need frequency of social contact, and doing stuff together is important too. Some of the grandparents I spoke with for this book visited their children and grandchildren as regularly as clockwork, others less often. To put it simply, 'associational solidarity' is about the extent to which people in the family feel connected to, and identify with, one another. Do they visit the same schools, clubs, churches, sports and social groups, organisations and communities? Spending time together is fundamental to human wellbeing, and people seek out and develop meaning from their membership of groups.

Associational solidarity involves generating a sense of belonging and a shared identity, offering mutual support and participating in shared activities. The Grandparenting Code says 90 per cent of grandparenting is about 'intelligently showing up', one way or another: being present at grandchildren's school functions, music, dance or drama performances, or perhaps volunteering at sporting events. Doing so generates a sense of purpose, social support and social identity within a family. It helps to build social capital and promote social cohesion, which in turn can lead to better individual and collective outcomes.

Consensual solidarity

The third component is what Silverstein and Bengtson call 'consensual solidarity'. This refers to whether the individuals in the broader family share similar values, beliefs and goals. It doesn't mean there needs to be total agreement between a child, their parents and their grandparents on every topic under the sun, but it says the bond is likely to be better and deeper where there are at least some shared values and beliefs, as these provide a platform for social cohesion.

In the context of grandparenting, consensual solidarity could refer to the degree to which grandparents and their adult children share similar values and beliefs about grandparenting, childrearing and family relationships. It involves a collective understanding of what is important, what is right and what is expected within the group, which is often guided by cultural or religious beliefs, political ideologies or shared experiences. It provides a framework for social interactions and relationships, enabling individuals to understand and predict the behaviour of others, based on their shared values and beliefs. Grandparents often feel great satisfaction when their family members support the same football team, for instance, vote for the same political party or are members of the same faith group.

Affectual solidarity

The fourth aspect is the quality of the connections we make, which Silverstein and Bengtson refer to as 'affectual solidarity'. This is about the intensity of the emotional bond between grandparents, their adult children and their grandchildren. When grandparents provide emotional support, care and guidance to their grandchildren, this can strengthen the emotional bonds between all generations and maintain positive family relationships. This type of solidarity can also provide a sense of purpose and meaning, as individuals feel connected to others and are able to contribute to the wellbeing of their wider network.

Functional solidarity

The last-but-one element, according to Silverstein and Bengtson, is 'functional solidarity'—another somewhat strange term, which refers to the extent to which people rely on one another for practical or instrumental support. The psychological boffins are talking about the tangible or practical assistance that a grandchild receives from grandparents to solve a problem or meet a specific need, for instance. This type of support can take many forms, including financial assistance, transportation, childcare, helping with household tasks, or providing information or advice. It might also involve the coordination of activities and responsibilities within the family, such as scheduling and planning for family events or holidays. Functional solidarity is not a one-way street, and it is common for grandparents to be both sources and beneficiaries of this kind of support: while some might look after their grandchildren, others might receive visits from their children to help with household tasks.

Normative solidarity

Finally, Silverstein and Bengtson talk about 'normative solidarity', or our sense of unity and mutual support—the strength of obligation and responsibility we feel towards other family members. This is based on shared values and norms within a particular community or society. It is characterised by a sense of mutual obligation to maintain these values and norms, and to support one another in doing so. Most of us have come across families that exhibit a strong belief in the need for and importance of family cohesion and assistance between family members.

Adding more love to the lineage

For the most part, the grandparents I interviewed for this book told me that nothing compared to the magic of watching their children metamorphose into loving, caring parents. This transition clearly brought them a sense of pride. And when their grandchildren arrived, their excitement, enthusiasm and willingness to help empowered them to add yet more love to their lineage.

The prominent Australian grandparents whose words are featured in this book make it clear that the relationship between a grandparent and a grandchild is special in multiple ways. They all see the connection across generations as unique and important. Grandparents have lived through events that their grandchildren may never experience, and they can share the wisdom and perspectives they gained through those times.

Grandparents often have a special bond with their grandchildren, and can offer an unconditional love and support that is different from that in the parent–child relationship. This can provide grandchildren with a sense of security and comfort, and help them develop and maintain a positive self-image.

Grandparents often have more time and energy to engage in playful activities with their grandchildren, and thus to foster a sense of joy and wonder in the child. Grandparents may also be more likely to indulge their grandchildren and spoil them a bit, which can create positive memories and experiences.

Most importantly, they can serve as mentors and guides for their grandchildren, offering advice and guidance as they navigate life's challenges. They can help instil important values and beliefs in their grandchildren and serve as positive role models.

Overall, the relationship between a grandparent and grandchild is based on love, respect and mutual admiration. It can provide emotional support, foster positive development and create lasting memories that will be cherished for a lifetime—but, sadly, it is also one that will inevitably end. In the next chapter we will look at the often difficult topic of death.

FOURTEEN

Saying goodbye

The death of a grandparent is often the first significant death a grandchild experiences. As a result, the conversations you have with the child before this occurs can change the colour and pattern of the way they perceive loss down the road.

As a psychologist who has been working with young people for over 30 years, it is evident to me that few families, let alone grandchildren, have any preparation for handling bereavement, nor are many adults equipped to support children at times of grief and personal loss. While attitudes towards loss and grief can vary across different cultures, and death's a fact of life, many in the Western world are actually not very good at acknowledging its psychological aftershocks.

This is partly due to the fact that the last 100 years have seen dramatic improvements in hygiene and sanitation, resulting in significant changes in life expectancy, and infant mortality. In Australia in 1900, just over 50 per cent of deaths were of children under fifteen, and our culture had no choice but to come to terms with death and dying.

Today, death and dying have become sanitised, moving from homes to hospitals and hospices. The idea of death makes us feel uncomfortable, and many grandchildren have had little exposure to it. Most of our grieving rituals have moved from the community to funeral homes and crematoriums. This denial is even reflected in our terminology for death: 'passed away', 'kicked the bucket', 'shuffled off'.

The public expects nothing less than perfect health, and the present generation does not expect to die, so death, when it does come, is all the more bitter for being seen as stealthy, unexpected and selective. For some, death is seen as an obscenity, an abomination, and it is within this context that grandchildren grieve.

So how can we help young people cope with saying goodbye? Researchers have studied children's understanding of death and dying and have identified three main sources of information that children access: direct exposure to death, parental communication about death, and depictions of death and dying in the media. Researchers have also found that children are thinking about these topics, even if they lack an adult vocabulary to express their thoughts about dying and death.

Grandparents can play an important role in shaping their grandchildren's understanding of death. From this psychologist's perspective, it makes sense for grandparents to talk with their grandchildren about this subject, which is universal but (in Western cultures particularly) largely avoided.

A good friend recently told me that death was one of the main themes of conversation between she and her granddaughters. 'By the time they were four,' she wrote to me, 'my granddaughters were asking about death. Who would die? How did you die? When would you die? Why would you die? We all have different versions of what happens, depending on our beliefs. My granddaughters know that I will become part of a star: Venus, the Evening Star. I will be there as the light of the day fades to shine down upon them, watch over them and love them. I have taught them that I am not afraid—that dying is just the last task I have to complete on my blessedly long journey into the cosmos.'

It makes sense that children direct their first death-related questions to their parents, who shoulder most of this responsibility, but grandparents have lived a long time and lost friends, and are well positioned to join the conversation.

If children are asking questions, it means they want to know. And if we avoid or change the subject, then the child is learning that it's a bad thing for them to ask about. Our aim should be to communicate clearly—at an age-appropriate level, of course—so that they begin to appreciate what death means: its universality and finality. Death is irreversible, it renders living things non-functional, and it happens eventually to everyone.

Children have their own unique concept of death, which is influenced by their age, emotional development, past experiences with death, and surroundings. While babies have no concept of death, they may react to separation from a parent or any change in their routine with grief.[1] Preschool children may have a cartoonish understanding of death—that you die and then pop up again—but as they get to primary school they start to understand the cycle of life and the pervasiveness of death.[2] Certainly by the age of eight to twelve most children have a more adult understanding, and this is when they may want to know details like what happens to our bodies after we die—at funerals, in cemeteries and so on. Be guided by their curiosity.

The thoughts and feelings that accompany people as they near the end of life can be overwhelming for adults and children alike. Grandparents understand that death is an unavoidable part of life, but talking about death and dying with children can make us feel uncomfortable.

For many children, the death of a grandparent is the first time they'll experience the passing of someone they love. They may already have experienced the death of a pet or another animal, which can mean they're somewhat familiar with the concept of death. If not, there are some fabulous children's books available that adults can use to help the young people in their lives prepare for the death of a much-loved grandparent.[3]

Here are some suggestions for how to talk to your cherished grandchildren about death and dying. Explaining death to kids can be a delicate and difficult task, and it's important to adjust explanations to the child's age and cognitive capacity. When describing death, use clear language and specific examples to show that the person's body has stopped functioning and they will no longer be able to perform the same actions they once could.

Be open and honest and avoid euphemisms or perplexing analogies, since they can increase uncertainty or dread. Some children might require time to process and comprehend the idea of death, so be ready to repeat yourself and respond to enquiries. It is okay to use simple metaphors or analogies that make death more understandable to young children. You may clarify, for instance, that just as flowers blossom and then wither, so too do other living things. Encourage them to express their feelings out loud and offer a secure setting for doing so.

As mentioned earlier, younger children may find it difficult to understand the permanence of death, so avoid words or phrases that could imply a brief absence or slumber. Make it clear that the person won't be returning and won't be able to feel or experience anything any longer. If your family holds any particular religious or spiritual views about death, you should include these in your explanation. Keep in mind that every child is different, and their perceptions of and responses to death may differ. Adapt your strategy to their specific need and offer continuing assistance as they process their feelings and come to terms with the loss.

How to say goodbye

For grandparents who are facing their own mortality, saying goodbye to a grandchild for the final time can be a difficult and emotional experience. Making a video for them or writing them a letter can be a powerful way to leave them with a positive and permanent memory of you. But if it's appropriate for a grandparent to say goodbye in person in the weeks or months ahead of their death, this might help the grandchild with the process of grieving and healing. Here are a few suggestions for how you might approach such a moment.

- Tell your grandchild how much you love them and how much they mean to you. 'I want you to know how much I love you and how much joy you have brought into my life. I am grateful for all the time we've spent together.' You might also recall a special occasion or experience you shared.
- If you would like to impart any wisdom to your grandchild, this is the time to do it. On my list: it's okay to make mistakes; trust your feelings; always be kind; follow your dreams; watch what you say; show compassion to those less fortunate; stay in school (unless there is a compelling reason not to); choose your friends wisely; always strive to make the world a better place; and never give up on what you believe in.
- You might like to offer your grandchild your blessings for a happy and successful life. You might say something like: 'I wish you all the happiness and success in the world, my dear grandchild.'
- Let your grandchild know that you will always be with them in their memories and in their hearts. If you have particular

religious beliefs—about the afterlife, for instance—feel free to share these with your grandchild.

Overall, our message to our grandchildren should be that losing someone you love is sad, but the tears we shed for another person are not a sign of weakness. Rather, they are the sign of a pure heart. Memento mori: remember that you must die, whether you like it or not. As the writer Ian Martin observed: 'You are grandparents now; the conveyor belt of death is chugging along, and you are the next to go, Sunshine.'[4] But having grandchildren and saying goodbye will help ease the pain.

FIFTEEN

The Grandparenting Code

Becoming a grandparent can alter the course of your life. There is an undeniable euphoria in loving your grandchildren and being loved in return, as well as in observing their development and seeing your own characteristics being passed to a new generation. But there are challenges along the way. That is why I have organised this advice into the twenty principles of what I have called the Grandparenting Code.

Grandparenting is not a one-size-fits-all proposition. The relevance of the Code will depend very much on what sort of grandparent you are: are you Traditional, Fun, Indulgent, Hands-Off or Mentoring, or some combination of these? There is no perfect grandparent, but there are some psychological principles that are worth articulating that apply to all of us.

Note too that there might be some circumstances in which, for a variety of reasons, the Code does not directly apply. But if you happen to be about to enter the second generation game, you may find this useful.

In summary:

1. Respond to the pregnancy news with unbridled joy.
2. Honour any request to keep news of the impending birth secret.
3. When your grandchild first comes home, wait to be invited over.
4. Don't give the new parents unsolicited advice.
5. Offer reassurance and encouragement.
6. Don't comment negatively on the name the parents choose for your grandchild.
7. Be positive when you meet the child, and be realistic about your feelings.
8. Spend one-on-one time with your grandchild, and play, if time allows.
9. Manage your grandchild's use of technology.
10. Don't engage in 'grandsharenting'.
11. Spoil your grandchildren—in consultation with their parents.
12. Handwrite cards and letters to your grandchild.

13. Remain neutral about how your grandchildren are raised—except in certain circumstances.
14. Have a developmental perspective when it comes to teenagers.
15. Double-down on your relationship with grandchildren in the face of parental separation and divorce.
16. Encourage your grandchild to talk about loss, grief and disappointment.
17. Celebrate your grandchild's identity.
18. Become an informed part of the therapeutic team helping the neurodiverse grandchild.
19. Help your grandchildren learn more about their family heritage.
20. Superglue the family by creating and fostering family rituals.

1. Respond to the pregnancy news with unbridled joy

The Grandparenting Code begins when you get the news that you are going to become a grandparent. In almost every situation, 'Congratulations!' is the only appropriate response—and this is especially true when the pregnancy is planned and/or wanted. Let your child and/or their partner know that you are looking forward to being a grandparent. If you are so inclined, offer a hug and a 100-kilowatt smile to convey your unbridled joy. Once they make the decision to have a baby, your only job is to treat this as good news. The theme is positivity, support and respect. Don't immediately bombard them with questions; they will tell you what you need to know.

2. Honour any request to keep news of the impending birth secret

It's vital to honour the wishes of the couple/person having the baby in relation to spreading the news. This can be a sensitive emotional time, especially for parents who might have experienced miscarriages or a sudden infant death. Waiting until they give you the green light to share the news is kind and respectful.

3. When your grandchild first comes home, wait to be invited over

It's particularly important not to turn up to the hospital/home until invited. No doubt you are extremely excited to meet your new grandchild as soon as they arrive. But when a person is recuperating from childbirth, a horde of family members descending can be stressful and exhausting. So back off. A newborn baby needs constant skin-to-skin contact with their mother, which aids with connection and bonding. Wait for the summons. There is no set time frame for when grandparents should visit their new grandchild. It ultimately depends on factors such as the parents' wishes, and the health and well-being of both the baby and the grandparents. To avoid causing problems, it's best to have an open and honest conversation with the parents to determine the best time for a visit.

4. Don't give the new parents unsolicited advice

During the profound journey that is pregnancy and the post-birth period, mothers and their partners often receive a deluge of spontaneous counsel from all directions. These days, even perfect strangers feel entitled to offer parenting advice to brand-new parents and it can be overwhelming, confusing and annoying. The role of a grandparent-to-be is to reduce the parents' stress, and they can do this by listening and not offering advice unless they are asked directly. Some new grandparents find themselves at odds with today's medical recommendations. New scientific evidence means that sleep practices, car-seat recommendations, breastfeeding information and bottle-feeding methods have all changed in the past 25 years. If the mother and/or their partner has questions about the pregnancy and/or the postnatal care, they'll ask. Unsolicited advice can be interpreted as criticism. If you respect this part of the Code, it increases the likelihood that your opinion will be sought, and you'll have more chance to have some influence later on. Remember that your grandbaby is not *your* baby. Avoid making passive-aggressive comments or posting articles that support your viewpoint. If you are slow to offer criticism or advice, you will most likely earn the respect of your children and increase the odds of your being solicited for advice in the future.

5. Offer reassurance and encouragement

For a first-time parent or someone who has previously lost a child through miscarriage or perinatal death, pregnancy can be a time filled with uncertainty and anxiety. If reassurance is sought, grandparents can help by reminding the mother and their partner that most pregnancies go smoothly and result in healthy babies, and that advances in medical technology have made it possible to detect and treat potential complications early on. There are also a raft of physical and emotional changes that women experience after having a baby—hormones and lack of sleep can really do a number on a new mother's psychology. Remind them that this is a major life transition. Tell them not to be afraid to ask for help, that it's okay to make mistakes, and to take care of themselves, physically and emotionally.

6. Don't comment negatively on the name the parents choose for your grandchild

When it comes to grandparents' involvement, there are some areas that are strictly off-limits, and that includes baby names. This is an area that, unless you're asked for your opinion, you really can't get involved with. Your initial response to being told the names the parents have selected will be remembered, so keep it neutral. Many grandparents have told me that, after initially disliking a name, they got used to it. If the name really grates on you, then there's nothing stopping you from inventing a nickname that can be your special name for your grandchild.

7. Be positive when you meet the child, and be realistic about your feelings

When you do get an invitation and can meet your grandchild for the very first time, you really should have only one response: 'What a beautiful baby!' Some grandparents told me that meeting each of their grandchildren for the first time was a happy event, while others admitted that the bonding didn't always happen right away. Some told me that they felt sad because the birth made them realise how old they were, and they worried about whether they would live to see their grandchild grow into an adult. Allow for all feelings, and find someone other than the child's parents to talk them through with. Also, resist the urge to stamp the child with your DNA; avoid making comments like: 'Look at those eyes—just like mine!'

8. Spend one-on-one time with your grandchild, and play, if time allows

Given that the special connection between grandparents and grandchildren has a very positive influence on children's development, try to spend as much time as possible one-on-one with each of your grandkids. Grandparents are a source of positive memories, but also provide an emotional safety net, a support system that can bolster young people's emotional and psychological wellbeing. Without the direct responsibilities of parenting, grandparents can offer love, guidance and stability. Also keep in mind the importance of play in the physical, social, emotional and cognitive development of the child. A one-on-one grandma or grandpa date can be an opportunity to form a deeper bond and create positive memories. As Joyce Allston said, 'Grandparents, like heroes, are as necessary to a child's growth as vitamins.'

9. Manage your grandchild's use of technology

Ultimately, decisions about whether to and how to regulate technology use among grandchildren should be made in consultation with their parents, taking into consideration the individual needs and dynamics of each family. But it is fair and reasonable for grandparents to have their own rules about screentime when the grandchildren are in their care.

10. Don't engage in 'grandsharenting'

'Grandsharenting' refers to grandparents sharing information, photos and updates about their grandchildren on social-media sites such as Facebook. This might include pictures of their grandchildren at play, updates on their milestones or other details about their daily lives. While posting this data can be a way for grandparents to share their joy and pride in their grandchildren, it also has implications for the children's privacy and security, now and into the future. Educate yourself about the risks of exposing your grandchildren to unwanted attention from strangers, having their personal information and images used for purposes beyond the control of their parents, and even damaging their reputation in the future.

11. Spoil your grandchildren—in consultation with their parents

Grandparents have a right to spoil their grandchildren. It's a key part of the magic in the relationship. But as we saw in

Chapter 4, you must consult with their parents about this, as excessive spoiling—such as going over the top, or giving gifts that are inappropriate or in conflict with the parents' values—can cause problems. Show moderation and be respectful. This means not giving gifts for no reason, especially extravagant gifts. Never go against the wishes or rules that your adult children have established for their children.

12. Handwrite cards and letters to your grandchild

It's a simple fact that handwritten letters and cards feel authentic and permanent, especially in this age of text messages and social-media posts, which are so quickly forgotten as newer ones appear. Each person's handwriting is unique, making a handwritten card a one-of-a-kind keepsake. Penning a letter to your grandchild allows you to reflect more deeply and express your thoughts and feelings in a more meaningful way.

13. Remain neutral about how your grandchildren are raised—except in certain circumstances

Bite your tongue when you have a differing opinion, or try to be supportive when your adult children make parenting choices that you don't agree with. Your job is to serve and not to interfere. Don't judge, criticise or disrespect the parenting style of your children and their partners, and only intervene in certain exceptional circumstances—and then in a manner that is supportive, appropriate and respectful.

My view is that rudeness, developmental delay and safety are three broad areas in which grandparents should consider speaking up. The decision to intervene should be based on several factors, including:

- *The nature of the issue*: Intervene only when there is a clear and significant problem that affects the wellbeing of the grandchild.
- *The relationship with the parents*: Before intervening, consider the nature of your relationship with the children's parents, and the level of trust and cooperation that exists between you.

- *The impact on the family*: Reflect on how intervention might affect other family members and the family dynamic.
- *The grandchild's perspective*: If they are old enough, take into account the grandchild's perspective; seek their input, if appropriate, before intervening.

In general, grandparents should approach any intervention with care, sensitivity and a willingness to work with the parents and other family members to find a solution that benefits everyone. Additionally, grandparents should consider seeking the advice of a professional counsellor or therapist if they are unsure how to proceed.

14. Have a developmental perspective when it comes to teenagers

Adolescence can be a tricky period for several reasons: it is a time when young people experience rapid physical growth and development (now earlier than ever) as well as emotional changes; struggle with feelings of insecurity, anxiety and self-doubt; try to find their place in the world and figure out who they are; and deal with peer pressure. It's also a period of increased independence, self-discovery and transition into adulthood. Having a charismatic adult, such as a grandparent, with a clear understanding of the developmental psychology of adolescents and who can communicate in a non-judgemental, supportive manner can make all the difference to their adolescent trajectory.

15. Double-down on your relationship with grandchildren in the face of parental separation and divorce

It's important that grandparents continue their relationships with the grandchildren during a divorce, as it can be a source of reassurance during a difficult transition. My clinical experience suggests that not all children will be affected by divorce in the same way, with some being more resilient than others. Either way, grandparents can play a critical role in helping grandchildren adjust to the situation by providing an emotional sanctuary at a time when their parents may be less emotionally available. Grandparents should be vigilant for telltale behavioural changes, trouble at school, emotional volatility, somatic symptoms and regression. They can create a calm environment, maintaining routines, actively listening and being a source of comfort, love and security.

16. Encourage your grandchild to talk about loss, grief and disappointment

Dealing with disappointment is a normal part of life, and young people are still developing coping skills. Grandparents can play a big role in helping children deal with despondency, by acknowledging their feelings and telling them it's okay to feel the way they do. Help them gain perspective, and encourage them to express their feelings through words, art or physical activity. Instead of trying to fix the situation, help them come up with solutions to the problem that caused their dejection in the first place. Sharing examples from your own life may help them find something positive in the situation.

17. Celebrate your grandchild's identity

Grandparents should educate themselves about LGBTQIA+ issues and terminology to better understand their grandchild's experience. Grandparents can provide a supportive and non-judgemental safe space for their grandchild, allowing them to express their feelings and experiences. While all family members ought to respect the child's privacy and not share information about them without their say-so, if asked, the grandparent might even advocate for their grandchild by speaking up and working with the parents to ensure that the child receives the support they need.

Using the grandchild's correct name and pronouns is an important way to show support and respect for their gender identity. Research has shown that gender-affirming care, which includes the use of preferred pronouns, is associated with better mental health outcomes, including reduced rates of depression and anxiety. By contrast, children who are not affirmed in their gender identity and who experience rejection or discrimination are at increased risk of negative mental health outcomes, including higher rates of depression, anxiety and suicidal ideation.

18. Become an informed part of the therapeutic team helping the neurodiverse grandchild

Assuming time and circumstances permit, grandparents can be a source of support, guidance and love for their neurodiverse grandchild by learning about their condition, so that they can better understand their needs and how to support them. They can also assist by exhibiting patience and understanding and providing emotional support, by being a sympathetic listening ear and offering words of encouragement. Grandparenting Code point 8—spending time together and building a strong relationship—can also mean providing respite care to exhausted parents, giving them a much-needed break and time to recharge. Grandparents can create a safe and predictable environment by establishing routine visits in which the adults celebrate the grandchild's strengths and accomplishments, which can help their self-esteem and confidence.

19. Help your grandchildren learn more about their family heritage

Where possible, grandparents should offer a link to a child's family history and cultural heritage. Family history, in the form of stories and memories, can be part of the structure on which children build their life and identity. As such, you have one of the most important roles in society: as the oldest living representative of your family, you are the subsequent generations' best link to the past, and can have a special role teaching family history. So, if possible, fulfil this role by visiting places of family significance, creating a photo wall and researching your family tree—and involve your grandchildren wherever possible. 'Grandchildren are the dots that connect the lines from generation to generation,' in the words of Lois Wyse.[1]

20. Superglue the family by creating and fostering family rituals

Grandparents should reinforce the importance of family rituals and help give meaning and value to major events. Rituals play a significant role in family life and provide a shared sense of identity and belonging within a family. They establish traditions, customs and practices that are unique to the family and contribute to a sense of togetherness and continuity across generations. They often involve shared activities and meaningful interactions that foster stronger connections between family members. Whether it's a weekly family dinner, holiday celebrations or bedtime routines, rituals provide regular opportunities for the various generations to come together, communicate and bond. In fact, family rituals are powerful organisers of family life that offer stability during times of stress. Rituals also help families navigate and mark significant life events and transitions, providing a framework for acknowledging and celebrating important moments such as birthdays, graduations, weddings and religious ceremonies.

Afterword

Old age gives many delicious insights, including learning to negotiate with ageing and developing a simple gratitude. Everyone reading this book will have a use-by date. Having written and researched this book, it seems clear to me that, for most people, the birth of a first grandchild triggers an epiphany which in hindsight hardly qualifies as a surprise at all. It's a blinding flash of realisation that the heartfelt, unconditional love you felt when your child was born is not unique after all. It turns out to be entirely replicable and is as limitless as our universe. After this initial awakening has subsided, it seems that a lovely mundanity, the repeated infinite daily love, is an equal sequel to the first wave of parenthood. The ease and tranquillity of it, the banality of hanging out, and the sense of familiarity with people from an uncertain future, turns out to be one of the best feelings of all.

I hope the twenty Grandparenting Code principles resonate with you and help you feel more confident about strengthening your relationship with your children and their partners, better able to form a bond with your grandchildren, and encouraged to enjoy the time you spend with them as they grow.

The Grandparenting Code, and this book as a whole, is all about empowering you to decide what your role will be and to clearly communicate what and how you are prepared to support the new parents. My advice is to start small and grow your involvement as relationships develop. Don't be a 'people pleaser' who just says yes to everything, and do bear in mind your existing commitments, your available resources, your physical and mental health, and the needs of your partner.

A grandparent is a little bit parent, a little bit teacher, and a little bit best friend, and grandchildren are God's way of compensating us for growing old.

Last but not least . . . congratulations, and enjoy your beautiful new grandbaby!

Dr Michael Carr-Gregg

Melbourne, 2023

Your grandchild record

Scan this QR code to find a copy online

Full name

....

Date of birth

....

Place of birth

....

Birth weight

....

Birth length

....

Blood group

....

First smile

....

First words

....

First steps

....

Nicknames for parents

....

Nicknames for siblings

....

Nicknames for grandparents

....

First pet

....

Funniest sayings

....

First school

....

First teacher

....

Acknowledgements

The American columnist Jay McInerney once said, 'Editors are a little like dentists—nobody likes to go to them, but you always feel better after you've been.' That is certainly the case with Tom Bailey-Smith. Writing a book on grandparenting was the idea of Tom and his colleagues at Allen & Unwin. I am grateful for Tom's patience and thoughtful suggestions, along with Julian Welch and Greer Gamble for their copious literary panel-beating and their allowing me the creative licence to develop a first-of-its-kind Australian Grandparenting Code. I am particularly beholden to Tom for his dogged pursuit of famous Australians, including his close family friend Eric Tweedale—a Wallabies legend. I'm also indebted to the many grandparents who have been kind enough to share their insights on grandparenting, especially those well-known Australian grandparents who, despite their busy lives, have actually committed pen to paper in these pages.

I am also appreciative of my many clients and their families who have helped me understand that a grandparent's love is like no other. It's the glitter glue that binds generations together. Thanks to my family: Therese, Christopher, Danielle, Rupert and Katie, for their interest and support, and a special shout-out to my many friends for their support as well, especially Rebecca Philpot, Brigitte Johnson, Susan McLean, Sue Cahill, Elida Brereton and Imogen Newell-Quinn.

Notes

Introduction

1 J. Chamie, 'Increasingly indispensable grandparents', *Yale Global*, 4 September 2018, archive-yaleglobal.yale.edu/content/increasingly-indispensable-grandparents

2 'The age of the grandparent has arrived', *The Economist*, 12 January 2023, www.economist.com/international/2023/01/12/the-age-of-the-grandparent-has-arrived

3 Australian Bureau of Statistics, *Household and families: Census*, 2021, www.abs.gov.au/media-centre/media-releases/2021-census-shows-changing-face-australias-6-million-families

4 G. Graham & S. Swinford, 'Financial support for grandparents who look after children', *The Telegraph* (UK), 18 August 2014, www.telegraph.co.uk/news/politics/11042376/Financial-support-for-grandparents-who-look-after-children.html; A. Buchanan & A. Rotkirch, 'Twenty-first century grandparents: global perspectives on changing roles and consequences', *Journal of the Academy of Social Sciences*, vol. 13, no. 2, 2018, doi.org/10.1080/21582041.2018.1467034

5 K. Emmerton, 'Mozo insight: Aussie grandparents contribute billions in Greycare hours', *Mozo*, 3 June 2018, mozo.com.au/family-finances/mozo-insight-aussie-grandparents-contribute-billions-in-greycare-hours

6 Australian Bureau of Statistics, 'Grandparents are the main providers of informal care for children of working parents', 28 April 2015, www.abs.gov.au/ausstats/abs@.nsf/lookup/4402.0Media%20Release1June%202014

Chapter 1

1 J.B. Yorgason, L. Padilla-Walker & J. Jackson, 'Nonresidential grandparents' emotional and financial involvement in relation to early adolescent grandchild outcomes', *Journal of Research on Adolescence*, vol. 21, no. 3, 2011, onlinelibrary.wiley.com/doi/abs/10.1111/j.1532-7795.2010.00735.x

Notes

2 American Psychological Association, 'Building your resilience', 2012, www.apa.org/topics/resilience/building-your-resilience

3 B. Kakulla, 'Grandparents are gamers, too—especially grandmothers', AARP, September 2022, www.aarp.org/pri/topics/technology/internet-media-devices/gaming-grandparents-survey

4 M. Danielsbacka, L. Křenková & A.O. Tanskanen, 'Grandparenting, health, and well-being: a systematic literature review', *European Journal of Ageing*, vol. 19, 2022, pp. 341–68, doi.org/10.1007/s10433-021-00674-y

5 V. Bordone & B. Arpino, 'Do grandchildren influence how old you feel?', *Journal of Aging and Health*, vol. 28, no. 6, 2016, doi.org/10.1177/08982643156189

6 V. Bordone & B. Arpino, 'Is there a rejuvenating effect of (grand)childcare? A longitudinal study on German data', *The Journals of Gerontology: Series B*, vol. 77, no. 2, 2022, pp. 446–55, doi.org/10.1093/geronb/gbab021

7 A. Fiske et al, 'Depression in older adults', *Annual Review of Clinical Psychology*, vol. 5, 2009, pp. 363–89, www.ncbi.nlm.nih.gov/pmc/articles/PMC2852580

8 Queensland Brain Institute, 'Memory and age', qbi.uq.edu.au/brain-basics/memory/memory-and-age

9 A. McSweeney, 'What can productivity figures tell us about working in later life?', *Centre for Ageing Better*, 6 November 2019, ageing-better.org.uk/blogs/what-can-productivity-figures-tell-us-about-working-later-life

10 K. Hawkes, J.F. O'Connell & N.G.B. Jones, 'Hadza women's time allocation, offspring provisioning, and the evolution of long postmenopausal life spans', *Current Anthropology*, vol. 38, 1997, pp. 551–77

11 E.O. Chung et al., 'The contribution of grandmother involvement to child growth and development: an observational study in rural Pakistan', *BMJ Global Health*, vol. 5, 2020, e002181

12 H. Lehti, J. Erola & A.O. Tanskanen, 'Tying the extended family knot: grandparents' influence on educational achievement', *European Sociological Review*, vol. 35, 2019, pp. 29–48; R. Sear & D. Coall, 'How much does family matter? Cooperative Breeding and the demographic transition', *Population and Development Review*, vol. 37, 2011, pp. 81–112

13 R. Sear & R. Mace, 'Who keeps children alive? A review of the effects of kin on child survival', *Evolution and Human Behavior*, vol. 29, 2008, pp. 1–18

14 J.K. Rilling, A. Gonzalez & M. Lee, 'The neural correlates of grandmaternal caregiving', *Proceedings of the Royal Society B*, vol. 288, no. 1963, November 2021

15 K. Hawkes, J.F. O'Connell, N.G. Blurton Jones, H. Alvarez & E.L. Charnov, 'Grandmothering, menopause, and the evolution of human life histories', *Proceedings of the National Academy of Sciences*, vol. 95, 1998, pp. 1336–9

Chapter 2

1 'Commentator mocked for saying parents should ask babies for consent to nappy change', 11 May 2018, *News.com.au*, www.news.com.au/lifestyle/parenting/kids/commentator-

mocked-for-saying-parents-should-ask-babies-for-consent-to-nappy-change/news-story/6f3c45120ef9de5dee3df81621715c1b

2 M.M. Mueller & G.H. Elder Jr., 'Family contingencies across the generations: grandparent–grandchild relationships in holistic perspective', *Journal of Marriage and Family*, vol. 65, no. 2, 2003, pp. 404–17

3 The Aboriginal and Torres Strait Islander peoples of Australia are incredibly diverse, with hundreds of different cultural and language groups, each with their own unique terms and traditions. Therefore, there is no single term that is used to refer to grandparents across all Aboriginal cultures.

4 It's worth noting that the specific terms used to refer to grandparents can vary depending on the iwi (tribe) or hapū (sub-tribe) within Māori culture. Additionally, some families may use different terms of endearment or nicknames for their grandparents that are not widely used outside of their family or community.

Chapter 3

1 Australian Institute of Health and Welfare, 'Australia's mothers and babies: method of birth', 14 December 2022, www.aihw.gov.au/reports/mothers-babies/australias-mothers-babies-data-visualisations/contents/labour-and-birth/method-of-birth

2 D. Pascali-Bonaro, 'Childbirth education and doula care during times of stress, trauma, and grieving', *Journal of Perinatal Education*, vol. 12, no. 4, 2003 Fall, pp. 1–7, www.ncbi.nlm.nih.gov/pmc/articles/PMC1595172; M.H. Walter, H. Abele & C.F. Plappert, 'The role of oxytocin and the effect of stress during childbirth: neurobiological basics and implications for mother and child', *Frontiers in Endocrinology*, vol. 12, October 2021, doi.org/10.3389/fendo.2021.742236

3 Johns Hopkins Medicine, '4 common pregnancy complications', www.hopkinsmedicine.org/health/conditions-and-diseases/staying-healthy-during-pregnancy/4-common-pregnancy-complications

4 E. Docherty, 'From Marigold to Romy: the baby names you'll be hearing a lot more of in 2023', *Mamamia*, 4 January 2023, www.mamamia.com.au/top-baby-names-australia-2023

5 G. Siahaan, A. Fell & M. McCrindle, 'Baby names Australia report 2023', McCrindle Research, 2023

6 Elon Musk and partner Grimes originally named their child X Æ A-12, but 'Æ' and '12' violated Californian law for not being part of the English alphabet, and the parents changed the name to X.

7 M. Karr, *The Liars' Club*, Viking, New York, 1995

8 M. Riley, 'The first year of parenthood: new parents and their sleep patterns', *Sleep Junkie*, 10 May 2023, www.sleepjunkie.com/new-parents-and-sleep

9 G. DelRosario, 'Moms need to sleep like a baby, too!', *Journal of the American Academy of PAs*, vol. 32, no. 9, September 2019, pubmed.ncbi.nlm.nih.gov/31460978

Notes

Chapter 4

1 S.M. Moorman & J.E. Stokes, 'Solidarity in the grandparent–adult grandchild relationship and trajectories of depressive symptoms', *The Gerontologist*, vol. 56, no. 3, June 2016, pp. 408–20, academic.oup.com/gerontologist/article/56/3/408/2605571

2 E.J. Sonuga-Barke & M. Mistry, 'The effect of extended family living on the mental health of three generations within two Asian communities', *British Journal of Clinical Psychology*, vol. 39, no. 2, 2000, pp. 129–41

3 Max Planck Institute for Human Development, 'Helping pays off: people who care for others live longer', 22 December 2016, www.mpib-berlin.mpg.de/press-releases/helping-pays-off

4 K. Burn & C. Szoeke, 'Grandparenting predicts late-life cognition: results from the Women's Healthy Ageing Project', *Maturitas*, vol. 81, no. 2, June 2015, pp. 317–22, www.sciencedirect.com/science/article/abs/pii/S0378512215006039; K.F. Burn, V.W. Henderson, D. Ames, L. Dennerstein & C. Szoeke, 'Role of grandparenting in postmenopausal women's cognitive health: results from the Women's Healthy Aging Project', *Menopause*, vol. 21, no. 10, October 2014, pp. 1069–74, pubmed.ncbi.nlm.nih.gov/24714623

5 J.K. Rilling, A. Gonzalez & M. Lee, 'The neural correlates of grandmaternal caregiving', *Proceedings of the Royal Society B*, vol. 288, no. 1963, 24 November 2021, royalsocietypublishing.org/doi/10.1098/rspb.2021.1997

6 C.S. Nave, R.A. Sherman, D.C. Funder, S.E. Hampson & L.R. Goldberg, 'On the contextual independence of personality: teachers' assessments predict directly observed behavior after four decades', University of California, Riverside; Oregon Research Institute & University of Oregon, 8 July 2010, rap.ucr.edu/naveetalSPPS.pdf

Chapter 5

1 S. Herculano-Houzel, 'The remarkable, yet not extraordinary, human brain as a scaled-up primate brain and its associated cost', *Proceedings of the National Academy of Sciences*, vol. 109, suppl. 1, 22 June 2012, pp. 10661–8, www.pnas.org/doi/10.1073/pnas.1201895109

2 M. Dix, 'Do babies have kneecaps?', *Healthline*, 27 March 2019, www.healthline.com/health/do-babies-have-kneecaps

3 S. Bradley, 'When do babies start crying tears?', *Healthline*, 31 July 2020, www.healthline.com/health/baby/when-do-babies-get-tears

4 Primary Care Pediatrics at Nemours Children's Health, 'Your bones', kidshealth.org/en/kids/bones.html

5 B. Kellogg, 'Birthmarks: when should parents be concerned?', *Nationwide Children's Hospital*, 3 May 2018, www.nationwidechildrens.org/family-resources-education/700childrens/2018/05/birthmarks-when-should-parents-be-concerned

6 D. Christiano, 'What it means if your baby is losing hair', *Healthline*, 22 October 2019, www.healthline.com/health/baby/baby-hair-loss

7 H. Bennett, 'Newborn reflexes: 5 instincts your baby is born with', *Today's Parent*, 6 January 2021, www.todaysparent.com/baby/baby-development/reflexes-5-instincts-your-baby-is-born-with

8 C. Pagano, 'When do babies first smile?', *Healthychildren.org*, 29 April 2021, www.healthychildren.org/English/tips-tools/ask-the-pediatrician/Pages/When-do-babies-first-smile.aspx

9 G. Dewar, 'How do babies respond to music in the womb?', *Parenting Science*, 2021, parentingscience.com/how-do-babies-respond-to-music-in-the-womb

10 Pamela Gerloff, 'You're not laughing enough, and that's no joke', *Psychology Today*, 21 June 2011, www.psychologytoday.com/au/blog/the-possibility-paradigm/201106/youre-not-laughing-enough-and-thats-no-joke

11 'Do babies have taste buds?', *SneakPeek*, 14 April 2021, sneakpeektest.com/blog/do-babies-have-taste-buds

12 Center on the Developing Child, 'The science of early childhood development', *Harvard University*, developingchild.harvard.edu/resources/inbrief-science-of-ecd

13 S.A. Kuczaj & H.C. Eskelinen, 'Why do dolphins play?', *Animal Behavior and Cognition*, vol. 1, no. 2, 2014, pp. 113–27, www.animalbehaviorandcognition.org/uploads/journals/2/03.Kuczaj_Eskelinen_Final.pdf; J.W.S. Bradshaw et al, 'Why do adult dogs play?', *Behavioural Processes*, vol. 110, January 2015, pp. 82–7, research-information.bris.ac.uk/en/publications/why-do-adult-dogs-play

14 D. Feldman, 'Children's play in the shadow of war', *American Journal of Play*, vol. 11, no. 3, 2019, files.eric.ed.gov/fulltext/EJ1220280.pdf; United States Holocaust Memorial Museum, 'Hidden children: daily life', *Holocaust Encyclopedia*, encyclopedia.ushmm.org/content/en/article/hidden-children-daily-life

15 'Physical activity for babies and children: why and how much', *Raisingchildren.net.au*, raisingchildren.net.au/toddlers/nutrition-fitness/physical-activity/physical-activity-how-much

16 'Play! It makes you smarter!', *Macaroni Kid*, 9 October 2018, national.macaronikid.com/articles/5bae53728b245377e657464f/play-it-makes-you-smarter

17 Boston Children's Museum, 'Play and problem solving', 21 November 2013, bostonchildrensmuseum.blog/2013/11/21/1639

18 T. Paes, 'Creativity and pretend play', *British Council*, www.britishcouncil.org/programmes/creative-play/creativity-pretend-play

19 Children's Museum of Sonoma County, 'The value of play to reduce stress in children', 28 August 2020, www.cmosc.org/playtime-reduces-stress-in-children

20 Y.V. Zhao & J.L. Gibson, 'Evidence for protective effects of peer play in the early years: better peer play ability at age 3 years predicts lower risks of externalising and internalising problems at age 7 years in a longitudinal cohort analysis', *Child Psychiatry & Human Development*, 14 June 2022, link.springer.com/content/pdf/10.1007/s10578-022-01368-x.pdf

21 A. Bustamante et al., 'The brain architects: building resilience through play', *Center on the Developing Child, Harvard University*, developingchild.harvard.edu/resources/podcast-resilience-play

22 R.P. Dalston & F. Luongo, 'Play may be a deeper part of human nature than we thought', *Scientific American*, 8 October 2019, www.scientificamerican.com/article/play-may-be-a-deeper-part-of-human-nature-than-we-thought

23 S.M. Siviy, 'A brain motivated to play: insights into the neurobiology of playfulness', *Behaviour*, vol. 153, no. 6–7, 2016, pp. 819–44, www.ncbi.nlm.nih.gov/pmc/articles/PMC5646690

24 I. Martin, '"Beautiful mundanity and quotidian love": my joy at being Grandpa', *The Observer*, 6 March 2022, www.theguardian.com/lifeandstyle/2022/mar/05/beautiful-mundanity-and-quotidian-love-my-joy-at-being-grandpa

25 L. Ehrenfeld, 'Benefits of board games for children and their families', *Child Development Clinic*, January 2022, www.childdevelopmentclinic.com.au/benefits-of-board-games-for-children-and-their-families.html

Chapter 6

1 Interactive Games & Entertainment Association, 'Australian games industry statistics', igea.net/faq/australian-games-industry-statistics

2 American Academy of Pediatrics, 'Screen time and children', February 2020, www.aacap.org/AACAP/Families_and_Youth/Facts_for_Families/FFF-Guide/Children-And-Watching-TV-054.aspx

3 J.E. Brand & J. Jervis, 'Connected by games', *Digital Australia 2022*, Interactive Games & Entertainment Association, Eveleigh, 2021, https://igea.net/wp-content/uploads/2021/10/DA22-Report-SUMMARY-FINAL-17-10-21.pdf

4 Australian Communications and Media Authority, 'Kids and mobiles: how Australian children are using mobile phones', June 2020, www.acma.gov.au/publications/2020-12/report/kids-and-mobiles-how-australian-children-are-using-mobile-phones

5 The Royal Children's Hospital Melbourne, 'Excessive screen time remains top health concern for parents, poll finds', 18 March 2021, blogs.rch.org.au/news/2021/03/18/excessive-screen-time-remains-top-health-concern-for-parents-poll-finds

6 eSafety Commissioner, 'Who we are', www.esafety.gov.au/about-us/who-we-are

7 N. Elias, G. Nimrod & D. Lemish, 'The ultimate treat? Young Israeli children's media use under their grandparents' care', *Journal of Children and Media*, vol. 13, no. 4, June 2019, www.tandfonline.com/doi/abs/10.1080/17482798.2019.1627228

8 Elias, Nimrod & Lemish, 2019

9 C. Knorr, 'Parents' ultimate guide to YouTube Kids', *Common Sense Media*, 12 March 2021, www.commonsensemedia.org/articles/parents-ultimate-guide-to-youtube-kids

10 I. Fadelli, 'Study draws new link between dopamine-based reward learning and machine learning', *Medical Xpress*, 27 July 2022, medicalxpress.com/news/2022-07-link-dopamine-based-reward-machine.html

11 Organization for Economic Cooperation and Development, 'Children in the digital environment', *OECD Digital Economy Papers*, no. 302, 8 January 2021, www.oecd-ilibrary.org/science-and-technology/children-in-the-digital-environment_9b8f222e-en;jsessionid=Rx0YiNcrmBdPcc-LdQBS6AeF.ip-10-240-5-100

12 Nominet, 'Parents "oversharing" family photos online, but lack basic privacy know-how', 5 September 2016, www.nominet.uk/parents-oversharing-family-photos-online-lack-basic-privacy-know

13 Australian Federal Police, 'AFP urges parents to protect children as they head back to school', 27 January 2021, www.afp.gov.au/news-media/media-releases/afp-urges-parents-protect-children-they-head-back-school

14 Mind Matters, 'Many parents ignore risks of posting kids' data online', 30 July 2019, mindmatters.ai/2019/07/many-parents-ignore-risks-of-posting-kids-data-online

15 eSafety Commissioner, www.esafety.gov.au

Chapter 7

1 P.D. McGorry, C. Mei, A. Chanen, C. Hodges, M. Alvarez-Jimenez & E. Killackey, 'Designing and scaling up integrated youth mental health care', *World Psychiatry*, vol. 21, no. 1, February 2022, onlinelibrary.wiley.com/doi/full/10.1002/wps.20938

2 Mass Cultural Council, 'Boston Youth Arts Evaluation Project: brief history of adolescence &youth development', massculturalcouncil.org/creative-youth-development/boston-youth-arts-evaluation-project/brief-history-of-adolescence-youth-development

3 M. Rowland, 'Why social media is making you compare and despair', *WellBeing*, 4 January 2020, www.wellbeing.com.au/mind-spirit/mind/45202.html

4 K.H. Choi & S.C. Park, 'An increasing tendency of precocious puberty among Korean children from the perspective of COVID-19 pandemic effect', *Frontiers in Pediatrics*, vol. 10, 2022, www.ncbi.nlm.nih.gov/pmc/articles/PMC9454605

5 D.F. Maron, 'Early puberty: causes and effects', *Scientific American*, 1 May 2015, www.scientificamerican.com/article/early-puberty-causes-and-effects

6 A. Ghorayshi, 'Puberty starts earlier than it used to. No one knows why.', *New York Times*, 19 May 2022, www.nytimes.com/2022/05/19/science/early-puberty-medical-reason.html

7 Parenting Research Centre, *Parenting Today in Victoria*, 2022, www.parentingrc.org.au/ptiv

8 P.R. Bahurekso, 'Average teens spent 7.7 hours per week in front of the mirror', *Medcom.id*, 14 September 2015, www.medcom.id/english/lifestyle-en/nbw6aw3N-average-teens-spent-7-7-hours-per-week-in-front-of-the-mirror

Chapter 8

1 J. Weiner, *Fly Away Home*, Atria Books, New York, 2010

2 W. Tuohy, 'Number of couples seeking separation advice soars during lockdown', *Sydney Morning Herald*, 7 June 2020, www.smh.com.au/national/number-of-couples-seeking-separation-advice-soars-during-lockdown-20200605-p54zzf.html

3 R.A. Gardner, *The Parental Alienation Syndrome: A guide for mental health and legal professionals*, Creative Therapeutics, Cresskill, New Jersey, 1998

4 S.R. Rappaport, 'Deconstructing the impact of divorce on children', *Family Law Quarterly*, vol. 47, no. 3, 2013, pp. 353–77

5 N. Ferguson, 'Children's contact with grandparents after divorce', *Family Matters*, no. 67, Autumn 2004, aifs.gov.au/sites/default/files/nf_0.pdf; M. Jappens & J. Van Bavel, 'Relationships with grandparents and grandchildren's well-being after parental divorce', *European Sociological Review*, vol. 35, no. 6, December 2019, pp. 757–71, doi.org/10.1093/esr/jcz033

Notes

Chapter 9

1 'Is Australia really getting gayer? How gay can we get?' *Courier-Mail*, 3 June 2015, www.couriermail.com.au/news/queensland/chinchilla/is-australia-really-getting-gayer-how-gay-can-we-get/news-story/99dd71f2177b9ac3913540827f945cc1; Susie O'Brien, 'Our rainbow society', *Herald Sun*, 14 May 2023

Chapter 10

1 J. Christensen, 'Judge gives grandparents custody of Ohio transgender teen', *CNN*, 16 February 2018, edition.cnn.com/2018/02/16/health/ohio-transgender-teen-hearing-judge-decision/index.html

2 Murdoch Children's Research Institute, 'Transgender youth health', www.mcri.edu.au/impact/a-z-child-adolescent-health/t-z/transgender-youth-health

3 'Leading the way in transgender healthcare', *Royal Children's Hospital Foundation*, 7 December 2021, https://www.rchfoundation.org.au/2021/12/leading-the-way-in-transgender-healthcare/

4 Harvard Divinity School, 'The third gender and Hijras', 2018, rpl.hds.harvard.edu/religion-context/case-studies/gender/third-gender-and-hijras; 'India recognises transgender people as third gender', *The Guardian*, 15 April 2014, www.theguardian.com/world/2014/apr/15/india-recognises-transgender-people-third-gender

5 A. Austin, S.L. Craig, S. D'Souza & L.B. McInroy, 'Suicidality among transgender youth: elucidating the role of interpersonal risk factors', *Journal of Interpersonal Violence*, vol. 37, nos 5–6, March 2022, pubmed.ncbi.nlm.nih.gov/32345113

6 J.C. Sorbara et al., 'Mental health and timing of gender-affirming care', *Pediatrics*, vol. 146, no. 4, October 2020, publications.aap.org/pediatrics/article/146/4/e20193600/79683/Mental-Health-and-Timing-of-Gender-Affirming-Care

7 Minus18, www.minus18.org.au

Chapter 11

1 Health Direct, 'Asperger's syndrome', November 2020, www.healthdirect.gov.au/aspergers-syndrome

2 Australian Institute of Health and Welfare, *Autism in Australia: web report*, last updated 5 April 2017, www.aihw.gov.au/reports/disability/autism-in-australia/contents/autism

3 P. Ratnayake, 'What is pathological demand avoidance (PDA) and how can we address it?', *Australian Childhood Trauma Group*, theactgroup.com.au/pathological-demand-avoidance

4 M. Sarris, 'When a grandchild has autism', *Simons Powering Autism Research*, 21 April 2023, sparkforautism.org/discover_article/grandchild-has-autism

5 D.A. Trevisan, M. Hoskyn & E. Birmingham, 'Facial expression production in autism: a meta-analysis', *Autism Research*, vol. 11, no. 12, December 2018, pp. 1586–601, pubmed.ncbi.nlm.nih.gov/30393953

6 T. Pedersen, 'Walking on tiptoes: is this a sign of autism?', *PsychCentral*, 7 November 2022, psychcentral.com/autism/walking-on-tiptoes-autism

7 J.H. Filliter et al., 'Positive affect in infant siblings of children diagnosed with autism spectrum disorder', *Journal of Abnormal Child Psychology*, vol. 43, August 2014, pp. 567–75, link.springer.com/article/10.1007/s10802-014-9921-6

8 J. Netting, 'Repetitive behavior in toddlers may signal autism', *Spectrum*, 20 March 2014, www.spectrumnews.org/news/repetitive-behavior-in-toddlers-may-signal-autism

9 L.J. Rudy, 'Lack of eye contact as a symptom of autism', *Verywellhealth*, 16 January 2023, www.verywellhealth.com/autism-symptoms-and-eye-contact-260565

10 L.J. Rudy, 'The reasons autistic children play differently', *Verywellhealth*, 15 May 2022, www.verywellhealth.com/autistic-child-form-of-play-259884

11 T. Attwood, 'Autism and anxiety', *Transforming Autism Project*, 29 January 2018, www.youtube.com/watch?v=Vqv8ByLeCz4

12 S. Deweerdt, 'Repetitive behaviors and "stimming" in autism, explained', *Spectrum*, 31 January 2020, www.spectrumnews.org/news/repetitive-behaviors-and-stimming-in-autism-explained

13 E. Spackman, L.D. Smillie, T.W. Frazier, A.Y. Hardan, G.A. Alvares, A. Whitehouse & M. Uljarevic, 'Characterizing restricted and unusual interests in autistic youth', *Autism Research*, vol. 16, no. 2, February 2023, pp. 394–405, pubmed.ncbi.nlm.nih.gov/36453155

14 M. Sarris, 'What do we know about noise sensitivity in autism?', *Kennedy Krieger Institute*, 15 June 2015, www.kennedykrieger.org/stories/interactive-autism-network-ian/noise-sensitivity-autism

15 C. Morrison, 'Do smell and taste sensitivities affect people with autism?', *ASD Today*, 13 January 2022, www.asdtoday.com/post/autism-smell-and-taste-sensitivities

16 A.R.B. Deolinda, 'Autism and picky eating: why do children on spectrum struggle with food?', *The Autism Site*, blog.theautismsite.greatergood.com/picky-eating

17 'History's 30 most famous people with autism', *Applied Behavior Analysis*, www.appliedbehavioranalysisprograms.com/historys-30-most-inspiring-people-on-the-autism-spectrum

Chapter 12

1 R. Fivush, M. Duke & J. Bohanek, '"Do you know . . .": the power of family history in adolescent identity and well-being', *Journal of Family Life*, 2010, www.journaloffamilylife.org/doyouknow.html

2 P. David et al, 'Grandparents embrace changing attitudes and technology', *American Association of Retired Persons*, April 2019, www.aarp.org/research/topics/life/info-2019/aarp-grandparenting-study.html

3 P. Collins, 'Anger as grandparents are dubbed "GRANDFRIENDS" at school events', *Daily Mail*, 3 November 2022, www.dailymail.co.uk/news/article-11384185/NSW-Anger-grandparents-called-grandfriends-school-events.html

4 V. Marian et al, 'Bilingualism: consequences for language, cognition, development, and the brain', *American Speech-language Hearing Association Leader*, vol. 14, no. 13, October 2009, leader.pubs.asha.org/doi/10.1044/leader.FTR2.14132009.10

Notes

Chapter 13

1 M. Silverstein & V.L. Bengtson, 'Intergenerational solidarity and the structure of adult child-parent relationships in American families', *American Journal of Sociology*, vol. 103, no. 2, September 1997, pp. 429–60, www.journals.uchicago.edu/doi/abs/10.1086/231213

Chapter 14

1 Stanford Medicine Children's Health, 'A child's concept of death', www.stanford childrens.org/en/topic/default?id=a-childs-concept-of-death-90-P03044
2 Children's Hospital of Philadelphia, 'A child's concept of death', www.chop.edu/conditions-diseases/childs-concept-death
3 I. Abedi, *Farewell, Grandpa Elephant: What happens when a loved one dies?*, Sky Horse, New York, 2012; N. Griffiths & G. Buckingham, *Grandma and Grandpa's Garden*, Red Robin Books, Langport, 2008; 'Books to help kids understand death and grief', *CareSearch*, www.caresearch.com.au/Portals/20/Documents/Dying2Learn/Dying2Learn_FactSheet_Childrensbooks.pdf
4 I. Martin, '"Beautiful mundanity and quotidian love": my joy at being Grandpa', *The Observer*, 6 March 2022, www.theguardian.com/lifeandstyle/2022/mar/05/beautiful-mundanity-and-quotidian-love-my-joy-at-being-grandpa

Chapter 15

1 Lois Wyse, *Funny, You Don't Look Like a Grandmother*, Harmony Publishing, California, 2011.

Resources

Websites for grandchildren and grandparents

They specifically cater to Australian children and provide resources, activities and information tailored to their needs. Here are some excellent websites for grandchildren:

- **Playgroup Australia** (www.playgroupaustralia.org.au): Playgroup Australia is a national organisation that promotes and supports playgroups for young children. Their website offers information on local playgroups, parenting tips, activity ideas and resources for grandparents to engage with their Australian grandchildren.
- **ABC Kids** (www.abc.net.au/abckids): ABC Kids is the children's programming division of the Australian Broadcasting

Corporation (ABC). Their website features a variety of educational games, videos and activities for children, including shows specifically produced for Australian kids.

- **Raising Children Network** (raisingchildren.net.au): The Raising Children Network is an Australian website that provides evidence-based parenting information and resources. It covers a wide range of topics, including child development, health, education, and activities suitable for Australian children of different ages.
- **Kids Helpline** (kidshelpline.com.au): Kids Helpline is a counselling service available to Australian children and young people. Their website offers resources, articles and support for kids on various topics such as mental health, bullying, relationships and general wellbeing.
- **National Gallery of Australia** (nga.gov.au): The National Gallery of Australia's website provides online art activities and resources for children. It includes virtual tours, interactive exhibits and art-making ideas to foster creativity and cultural understanding in Australian children.
- **Australian Geographic** (www.australiangeographic.com.au/kids): Australian Geographic's Kids website offers educational content, nature exploration ideas, quizzes and games designed to engage and educate children about Australian wildlife, geography and culture.

- **State Library of Queensland** (https://www.slq.qld.gov.au/discover/children-and-families): The State Library of Queensland's kids website offers reading recommendations, online storytelling sessions and interactive activities for children to explore literature, storytelling and Queensland's cultural heritage.

Below are some overseas websites I have found to be brilliant. They offer a range of resources and support for grandparents, whether they are seeking information, looking for activities to do with their grandchildren or seeking connections with other grandparents.

- **American Association of Retired Persons** (www.aarp.org): AARP is a non-profit organisation dedicated to empowering older adults. Their website offers a wealth of resources for grandparents, including articles and advice on health, finances, travel and caregiving.
- **Grandparents.com** (www.grandparents.com): A comprehensive website designed for the older generation. It features articles, activities, recipes, travel tips, and forums where grandparents can connect and share experiences.

- **Generations United** (www.gu.org): Generations United is an organisation that promotes intergenerational connections and supports the wellbeing of children, youth and older adults. Their website provides resources for grandparents raising grandchildren, including legal information, support groups and educational materials.
- **Legacy Project** (www.legacyproject.org): The Legacy Project is dedicated to passing down wisdom from older generations to younger ones. Their website offers activities, ideas and resources for grandparents to connect with their grandchildren and share their experiences and values.
- **Grandkids Matter** (www.grandkidsmatter.org): Grandkids Matter is a website that focuses on the importance of grandparent–grandchild relationships. It provides resources, articles and ideas for building strong connections with grandchildren and having a positive impact on their lives.

Popular genealogy websites

- **Ancestry** (www.ancestry.com.au): This website offers access to a vast collection of online records and resources, allowing individuals to trace their family history and explore their roots.

- **MyHeritage** (www.myheritage.com): A website that provides access to billions of historical records and family trees, as well as to DNA-testing services. It also allows users to create and share family documents and photos.
- **FamilySearch** (www.familysearch.org): A free website provided by the Church of Jesus Christ of Latter-day Saints that offers access to a large collection of genealogical records and resources, including census records, military records, and birth and death certificates.
- **Findmypast** (www.findmypast.com.au): A genealogy website that specialises in records from the UK and Ireland, offering access to more than 9 billion historical records, including census records, military records and newspapers.
- **23andMe** (www.23andme.com/en-int): A DNA-testing and ancestry service that provides information about an individual's genetic ancestry, health and traits.
- **Archives** (www.archives.com): A subscription-based genealogy website that offers access to millions of historical records, including census records, vital records and military records.

Note: Before using services like these, read the fine print and make sure you understand the privacy policies of the company before submitting a DNA sample.

Books on grandparents for children

- *My Nanna is a Ninja* by Damon Young: This delightful picture book celebrates the special bond between a grandchild and their grandmother, who happens to be a ninja. It's a fun and heartwarming story that showcases the unique qualities and adventures grandparents can bring to a child's life.
- *Grandma Wombat* by Jackie French and Bruce Whatley: This gorgeous book follows the mischievous Grandma Wombat as she embarks on hilarious and unconventional adventures with her grandchild. It's a humorous and endearing tale that captures the spirit of grandparent–grandchild relationships.
- *What Do You Call Your Grandma?* and *What Do You Call Your Grandpa?* by Ashleigh Barton and Martina Heiduczek are charming and uplifting books that celebrate the many different ways we say grandma and grandpa.
- *Granny McFlitter the Champion Knitter* by Heather Haylock and Lael Chisholm: This rhyming story follows the adventures of a penguin-rescuing grandmother. It's full of heart, humour and whimsical characters.
- *Grandpa's Big Adventure* by Paul Newman: In this entertaining picture book, a young girl and her grandfather set off on a grand adventure together. They embark on imaginative

journeys and create lasting memories, highlighting the joy of spending time with grandparents.

- *Grandma's Guide to Happiness* by Andrew Daddo and Stephen Michael King. A beautifully illustrated book celebrating the magic of grandmotherly philosophy, it emphasises the wisdom, guidance and unique perspectives that grandparents can provide.
- *The Grandad Tree* by Trish Cooke and Sharon Wilson: This touching story follows a young boy who visits his granddad's tree every summer. As the boy grows older, the tree and his granddad remain constant sources of comfort and love, reminding readers of the enduring bond between grandparents and grandchildren.

Websites for adolescents and their carers

These websites offer a wealth of information, support and opportunities for Australian teenagers to navigate various aspects of their lives, including mental health, education, careers, relationships and social issues. They provide a platform for learning, connection and personal growth, helping teenagers make informed decisions and build a brighter future.

- **ReachOut** (au.reachout.com): An online mental health organisation that provides support, information and resources for young people. Their website offers articles, forums, self-help tools and professional advice on various topics, including mental health, relationships and study stress.
- **Youth Central** (www.youthcentral.vic.gov.au): A Victorian Government website that offers a wide range of information and resources for Australian teenagers. It covers topics such as education and career guidance, study tips, job-hunting advice, volunteering opportunities and life skills.
- **headspace** (headspace.org.au): Australia's National Youth Mental Health Foundation. Their website provides valuable information, resources and support for young people dealing with mental health issues, including articles, fact sheets, self-help tools and access to professional support services.
- **Student Edge** (studentedge.com.au): An Australian membership-based website that offers a range of resources and opportunities for students and young people. Members gain access to exclusive discounts, scholarships, job listings, study tips and articles on various topics related to student life.
- **National Youth Week** (www.youthcoalition.net/national-youth-week): An annual celebration of young people in Australia. Their website provides information about

upcoming events, activities and opportunities for Australian teenagers to engage with their communities, showcase their talents and participate in youth-focused initiatives.

- **The Line** (www.theline.org.au): A website that promotes healthy relationships and respectful behaviour among young people. It offers information, tools and resources to help Australian teenagers navigate issues such as consent, communication, relationships and gender equality.
- **The Smith Family** (www.thesmithfamily.com.au): A national charity organisation in Australia that supports disadvantaged students and their families. Their website provides educational resources, scholarships, mentoring programs and career guidance to help young Australians from disadvantaged backgrounds achieve their potential.
- **Australian Youth Climate Coalition** (www.aycc.org.au): A movement of young people passionate about addressing climate change. Their website offers resources, campaigns and opportunities for Australian teenagers to get involved in climate activism, sustainability initiatives and environmental advocacy.

Some of the best websites for youth mental health in Australia

Mental health issues are a significant concern for teenagers in Australia, and it's important that the adults in their lives are aware of the resources where they can find the appropriate support.

- **headspace** (headspace.org.au): headspace is the National Youth Mental Health Foundation in Australia. It provides a wide range of services and resources for young people aged twelve to 25, including online counselling, information on mental health issues, self-help tools and access to local support services.
- **ReachOut** (au.reachout.com): A leading online mental health organisation for young people in Australia. It offers a wealth of information, tools and resources to support young people's mental health and wellbeing. It covers topics such as stress, anxiety, depression and relationships, and provides forums for peer support.
- **ReachOut Schools** (schools.au.reachout.com): Provides mental health and wellbeing resources for schools and educators in Australia. The website offers evidence-based

programs, lesson plans and tools to support the wellbeing of students, including resources specifically designed for young people.

- **Beyond Blue** (www.youthbeyondblue.com): A well-known Australian mental health organisation that provides support and information on depression, anxiety and other mental health concerns. Their youth-focused website offers resources specifically tailored to young people, including personal stories, fact sheets and online forums.
- **Kids Helpline** (kidshelpline.com.au): A free, confidential 24/7 helpline for children and young people in Australia. Their website offers a range of resources, articles and tools on various mental health issues, as well as the option to chat online with a counsellor or call their helpline.
- **eheadspace** (www.eheadspace.org.au): eheadspace is the online counselling service provided by headspace. It offers free, confidential support and counselling to young people aged twelve to 25 through online chat, email or phone. The website also provides information on mental health topics and self-help resources.

Support and resources for parents and grandparents of neurodiverse children in Australia

These websites can be valuable sources of information, guidance and support for parents of neurodiverse children in Australia. They offer resources, articles, webinars, helplines and connections to support networks that can assist parents in understanding their child's needs and accessing appropriate help and interventions.

- **Autism Awareness Australia** (www.autismawareness.com.au): A national organisation dedicated to promoting awareness and understanding of autism spectrum disorder (ASD). Their website provides information, resources and support for parents of children with autism.
- **Autism Spectrum Australia (Aspect)** (www.autismspectrum.org.au): Aspect is one of the largest service providers for people on the autism spectrum in Australia. Their website offers a range of resources, including information for parents, webinars, workshops and online courses.
- **Raising Children Network's Autism Hub** (raisingchildren.net.au/autism): Raising Children Network is a comprehensive

parenting website that includes a dedicated Autism Hub. It provides evidence-based information, practical tips and personal stories for parents of children with autism.

- **Amaze** (www.amaze.org.au): Amaze is an autism advocacy organisation based in Victoria, Australia. Their website offers resources and support for parents and carers of autistic children, including information on diagnosis, early intervention, education and transition to adulthood.
- **Learning Difficulties Australia** (www.ldaustralia.org): Provides information and support for parents of children with learning difficulties. Their website offers resources, articles and information on various learning difficulties, assessment and intervention strategies.
- **Association for Children with a Disability** (acd.org.au): A Victoria-based organisation that supports families of children with disabilities, including neurodiverse children. Their website provides resources, information and support services for parents across different disability areas.

Index

ABC Kids 256–7
adaptability 53
adolescence 113–14
  attention span 123
  autonomy 110–11, 127, 201
  brain changes 120–2
  communication tips 122–8
  developmental perspective 220, 230–1
  developmental psychology 114–15, 231
  early 116
  experimentation 122, 127
  life lessons 128
  meaning 114
  middle 117–18
  parents, relationship with 117, 120, 122, 127
  peer pressure 127
  physical changes 115–16
  play activities 82–4
  'precocious puberty' 115–16
  travelling with 119, 126
  websites 263–4
advice, unsolicited 110, 219, 222–3
adviser role 61, 110, 219
affectual solidarity 206
Albania
  sworn virgins 162
alienation
  grandparent 134–5, 139
  parental 133–4, 138
'allomothers' 14
alloparental effects 15
Allston, Joyce 226
Alzheimer's disease 52
Amaze 168
American Association of Retired Persons 194, 258
American Psychological Association 5
anaemia, postpartum 43

Index

Ancestry 193
anxiety disorders 172
arts and crafts
older children 83
toddlers and young children 82
asexual/aromantic 146
Asperger's syndrome 173
Association for Children with a Disability 268
associational solidarity 204–5
attention deficit hyperactivity disorder (ADHD) 172
Attwood, Tony 174
Australian Geographic 257
Australian Youth Climate Coalition 264
Autism Awareness Australia 267
Autism Spectrum Australia (Aspect) 267
autism spectrum disorder (ASD) 172, 173
avoiding interaction 179
behaviours 179
create a safe place 185
diagrams 185
identify triggers 183
interests of child 184
LFA 186
movie characters 177–8
panic 182
PDA and 176, 178
preferences and sensitivities 183–4
prevalence 175, 185
repetitive behaviours 180
response to diagnosis 175–6
sensory play 180
sensory sensitivities 174, 181, 184
signs 174–5
speak normally 184
'spectrum' 174, 185–6
strategies for grandparenting 182, 186
support and resources 267–8
autonomy 110–11, 127, 201

babies *see also* grandchild/ren
birth *see* birth of grandchild/ren
fun facts about newborns 73
mirrors 80
'peekaboo' 80
playing with 79
sensory toys 80
singing and talking 80
tummy time 79
unsolicited advice 219, 222–3
Baby Boomers xii
baby names 39–40, 219, 224
most popular 39
SBNs 39
behaviour
ASD *see* autism spectrum disorder (ASD)
disrespectful 66–7, 229
gender nonconforming 166
PDA 178
screentime and 101–2
Bengtson, Vern L. 202–206
bereavement *see* death

Index

Beyond Blue 266
bilingualism 197
bipolar disorder 172
birth of grandchild/ren
  common complications 42–3
  expressing opinions 24–5
  mother-to-mother support 35–6
  pre-birth activities 29, 32
  presence 35
bisexual 146, 160
blood clots, postpartum 43
board games 81, 83
  benefits 84
  popular 85
books
  choice for children 18–19
  grandparents, about 261–2
  toddlers and young children 82
brain development
  early adolescence 116–17
  neural connections 72–3
  'neurological ping-pong' 74
  play and 74, 78
  screentime and 96
  teenagers 120–2

Caro, Jane xviii, 76, 87–8
'charismatic adult' 3, 4, 6, 127–9, 231
Child Care Subsidy 12
child psychology
  adolescence 114–15
  Kauai Longitudinal Study 2–4
  parental alienation and 133–5
  resilience 1, 3, 56, 70
childcare
  average hours xiii
  communication 75–6
  grandparent health, link with 9–10, 58
  informal, provider of xiii–xiv
cisgender 153, 159
cocooning 40–1
coming out 147–9
  reactions to avoid 152–4
  suggested response 149–50, 153
communication
  brevity 123
  childcare expectations 75–6
  descriptive praise 125
  grandchild-parent conflict 68–9, 122
  humour 123
  positive feedback 124–5
  screen use 103
  selective comments 126–7
  separation and divorce 137
  talk less, listen more 122–3
  teenagers 120, 122
  ultimatums, avoiding 124
'compare and despair' phenomenon 115
conflict
  alienation *see* alienation
  communication with parents 68–9
  estrangement *see* estrangement
  grandchild-parent 63–5, 117, 120, 122, 127
  intervention 65–6, 229
  mediator role 117, 129, 143

Index

neutrality 142–3, 220, 229–30
teenagers 120, 122
connection 5, 135, 208
loss *see* estrangement
consensual solidarity 205–6
consultant role 61–3
cooking or baking 83, 111
cortex 78
frontal 121
criticism 111, 125, 229
cultural background, celebrating 196–7
cybersafety
'grandsharenting' 104–8, 219, 227
'sharenting' 104, 105
teaching 108–9

Dalai Lama 57
'deadnaming' 169
death 210
approaches to saying goodbye 215–17
child's concept 213
conversations 212–14
denial and discomfort 210–11
euphemisms or analogies 214
explaining to children 214–15
information sources for children 211–12
letter or video 215
memento mori 217
role of grandparents 212
sanitised 211
terminology 211
depression
elderly people 13
neurodiversity 172
postpartum 42
developmental delays 67–8, 229
digital photos 105–8
digital reputation 107
disrespectful behaviour 66–7, 229
distance from grandchild 34, 53, 62, 84–5, 203
divorce *see* separation and divorce
dopamine 121
DVDs 98
dyslexia 172
dyspraxia 172

eheadspace 266
elderly people
assumptions about 13–14
caregiver role 11
depression 13
doting and indulgent 10–11
financial support 12
health advantages of caring for grandchild 9–10, 58
modern technology and culture 8–9
myths 6–7
old, frail and sedentary 7–8
emotional empathy 15
employment 8
energy
grandchild 81
grandparent 75, 76, 209
eSafety Commission 93–4, 108–9

Index

estrangement 135, 138–9
  care for self and partner 141
  diarising 141
  grief 139
  new activities and interests 141
  support group 140
  talking 139–40
experience, value of 119–20

FaceTime 34, 62
family
  breakdown *see* separation and divorce
  heritage 196–7, 220
  history *see* genealogy
  rituals 236, 220, 235–6
  role model 17
  size xii
family narrative 191
Family Tax Benefit 12
family tree 193, 235
financial support 12
'foetal attraction' 21
food
  ASD and 181
  cooking or baking 83, 111
  treats 61
French, Jackie xviii, 18–19
Fröbel, Friedrich 86
'Fun Grandparents' 10, 218
functional solidarity 206–7

games *see also* play
  board 81, 83, 84–6
  outdoor 81
  video 8–9, 61, 83, 98
gaming consoles 89, 90 *see also* screentime
gay 146, 160
gender
  concept 159
  cisgender 153, 159
  identity 153, 160, 233
  multiple, cultural recognition of 161–2
  non-binary 159–60, 162
  therapy 157
  transgender *see* transgender grandchild/ren
gender-affirming care 169
gender dysphoria 163
gender-diverse 159, 162, 164, 165
gender nonconforming behaviour 166
genealogy
  curate images of family members 192–3
  PPTS mnemonic 191
  research family history 193
  responsibility 198
  revisit significant locations 192
  role of grandparents 189–91, 235
  share memories 193–4, 195
  websites 259–60
Generation Alpha xii
Generations United 258–9
German Ageing Survey 9
giftedness 172

Index

gifts and treats
  age-inappropriate 60–1, 228
  dilemma 59–60
  edible 61
  excessive 60, 228
  incompatible with parents' values 61, 228
grandchild record 197–8
grandchild/ren
  adaptability 53
  babies *see* babies
  benefits of relationship 52, 69–70
  'best interests', family law disputes and 136
  'bids' to engage 74
  bilingual 197
  bond with 50, 52, 54–6, 69, 206
  brain development *see* brain development
  closeness of relationship 202–3
  cocooning newborn 40–1
  conflict with parents *see* conflict
  criticism 111, 125, 229
  developing relationship 50
  developmental delays 67–8, 229
  digital reputation 107
  disrespect 66–7, 229
  divorce, effects of 137, 138
  document and record milestones 55
  drifting away from 201–2
  emotional care and wellbeing xiv, 52, 138
  estrangement 135, 138–41
  family history *see* genealogy
  find out their 'thing' 54–5
  first days 41–4
  first meeting 219, 225
  first visit 37–8, 219, 221–2
  'foetal attraction' 21
  gender identity 153, 160
  genetics 72
  'grandsharenting' online images 55, 104–8, 219, 227
  honesty 47–9
  identity formation 54, 118
  influence of grandparent xi, 109, 223
  intergenerational self 191
  learning machine 74–5
  legal guardian 12
  letter to unborn 29, 32
  LGBTQIA+ *see* LGBTQIA+ grandchild/ren
  'minimal encouragers' 58
  mutual respect 110, 112, 118
  names 39–40, 219
  neurodiverse *see* neurodiverse grandchild/ren
  one-on-one time 56–8, 63, 119, 219, 225–6
  personality *see* personality
  playing with *see* play
  primary carer of xii, 11, 58–9
  reading with 18–19, 53, 82
  screentime *see* screentime
  self-minimising behaviour 53
  sexual orientation 153, 160
  social and emotional competencies 4

Index

special occasions 55
spoiling 59–62, 219, 227–8
support from or to 207
teenagers *see* adolescence
transgender *see* transgender grandchild/ren
trust 110, 112
verbal fluency 53
websites 256–8
wellness 5
grandfather
cultural terminology 28–9, 30–1
'grandpa dates' 57
stereotype 7
Grandfriends Day 194, 196
Grandkids Matter 259
grandmother
birth of grandchild, presence at 35–6
cultural terminology 28–9, 30–1
direct care 14–15
'grandma dates' 57
neurobiology of caregiving 15
orca studies 51
Pakistan 15
stereotype 7
'Grandmother Effect' 14–15
Tanzania 14, 16–17
grandparent/s
alienation 134–5, 139
alloparental effects 15
anxiety xv
attentive, benefits of 74
benefits 52–4
'charismatic adult' 3, 4, 127–9
childcare see childcare
'classic' xiii
common questions xvii
connection 5, 135, 208
consultant or non-judgemental adviser 61–3, 110, 128, 219
contribution xiii, xv, 13
credibility 70
death *see* death
emotional care xiv, 52, 138
energy 76
family historian 190–1 *see also* genealogy
family law matters *see* separation and divorce
financial support 12
'Fun Grandparents' 10, 218
grandchild's greatest fan 124–5
'Hands-Off Grandparents' 10, 218
'Indulgent Grandparents' 10, 218
influence xi, 4
involvement, benefits of 50–1, 69
legal rights 136–7
life expectancy xi
long distance 34, 53, 62, 84–5, 203
mediators 117, 129, 143
'Mentoring Grandparents' 10–11, 218
mutual respect 110, 112, 118
myths 6–12
own needs 75–7
playing with grandchild *see* play
posting images online 55, 104–6

Index

presence 4
primary carer xii, 11, 58–9
proactive or reactive xvi
proportion of population xi, xii
relationship with grandchild *see* grandchild/ren
role 4, 17, 54, 75, 143, 209
separated 130–1
stereotypes 6–7
support xv, 17, 46, 207
teachers 50, 108–9
'Traditional Grandparents' 10, 218
transition xx, 20–1
values and beliefs, shared 205–6, 207
wisdom and skills, passing on 56, 129, 216
working 8
Grandparent Child Care Benefit 12
grandparenting
communication tips *see* communication
conflict, dealing with *see* conflict
mistake 21
myths *see* elderly people
strategies for grandchild with ASD 182–5
styles 10–11
websites 258–9
Grandparenting Code xviii, 21, 201, 218–19
birth of grandchild 37
developmental perspective on adolescence 220, 230–1
developing relationship with grandchild 53
disrespect 66, 229
family heritage 220, 235
family photos 192, 235
first meeting grandchild 219, 225
first visit with grandchild 37–8, 219, 221–2
grandchild-parent conflict 64–5, 219, 229–30
'intelligently showing up' 204
letter or card writing 63, 219, 228
LGBTQIA+ issues and terminology 220, 233
manage use of technology 219, 226
name preference 28–9
neurodiverse grandchild 220, 234
one-on-one time with grandchild 57, 219, 225–6
online safety 105
own needs 75, 76
pass on stories and information 189
play 86, 226
pre-birth activities 29, 32
pregnancy news 23–4, 219, 220–1
reassurance and encouragement to parents 219, 223–4
relevance 218
screentime 94, 95, 96, 109
separation and divorce 138, 231–2
spoiling grandchild 59–62, 219, 227–8
summary of principles 219–20
talking about loss, grief and disappointment 220, 232

Index

grandparenting superglue xiii, 203, 220, 235–6
Grandparents Australia 140
Grandparents.com 258
Grandparents Day 194
Grandparents Rearing Grandchildren 140
grandsharenting 55, 104, 219, 227
  dangers 105
  tips 105–8
'greycare' xiii
guardianship 12

Hadza people 14, 16–17
'Hands-Off Grandparents' 10, 218
Hawkes, Kristen 16
headspace 263, 265
health *see also* mental health
  caring for grandchild and 9–10, 52, 69
healthy thinking 5
high IQ 172
humour 123

identity
  associational solidarity and 204
  celebrate 220
  formation 54, 118
  gender 153, 160, 233
  LGBTQIA+ 149
  neurodiverse 173
  stories 193–4
  transgender 165–7

India
  Hijra 161
  transgender, recognition of 158
'Indulgent Grandparents' 10, 218
influence
  grandparents xi, 109, 223
  parental xi
intergenerational self 191
intergenerational solidarity 202–3
  affectual solidarity 206
  associational solidarity 204–5
  consensual solidarity 205–6
  functional solidarity 206–7
  normative solidarity 207–8
  structural solidarity 203
internet
  controlling use 103–4
  image sharing *see* 'grandsharenting'
  safety *see* cybersafety
internet addiction 98–100 *see also* screentime
intersex 146
'island of competence' 3, 54

Jagger, Mick 8

Kauai Longitudinal Study 2–4
'kaumātua' xviii
Kee, Jenny xviii, 110–12
Kids Helpline 257, 266
'kuia' xviii

learning 119
Learning Disabilities Association of Australia 268

Index

Legacy Project 259
legal rights 136–7
lesbian 145, 160
letter writing 63, 142, 215, 219, 228
LGBTQIA+ grandchild/ren xix, 144–5, 233
  ally 151
  coming out *see* coming out
  love and acceptance 154–5
  meaning of initialism 145
  mental health challenges 155
  population 147
  guide to rainbow terms 145–6
  stigma and discrimination 148, 164, 233
  transgender *see* transgender grandchild/ren
The Line 264
lobes, frontal and parietal 121
loss and grief
  death *see* death
  family breakdown 135–6, 139
  talking with grandchild 220, 232
love 33, 129, 154–5, 208–9
low-functioning autism (LFA) 186

Mackay, Hugh xviii, 130–1
Māori culture xviii–xix
Martin, Ian 80–1, 217
mastitis 42
McLean, Susan 105–6
meaning 6
memento mori 217
memories
  oral history record 195
  sharing 193–4
memory, age-related changes 13
mental health
  depression 13, 42
  internet addiction 100
  LGBTQIA+ people 155
  raising children, impact of 58
  relationship with grandchild 69
  suicidality 164
  transgender people 164, 233
  websites 265–6
'Mentoring Grandparents' 10–11, 218
'minimal encouragers' 58
mothers *see also* parents
  'allomothers' 14
  bleeding, postpartum 42
  blood clots, postpartum 43
  communication with *see* communication
  mastitis 42
  mother-to-mother support 35–6
  perineal tearing 42
  PPD 42
  pregnancy care, opinions about 24–5

name preference 28–9
National Gallery of Australia 257
National Youth Week 264
Native American two-spirit people 161
Nattrass, Stuart 51

Index

needs, own 75–7
neurodiverse grandchild/ren xix, 171, 220, 234
  conditions 172
  identity 173
  'neurodiverse' concept 171
  support and resources 267–8
neurodiversity movement 171–2
neutrality 142–3, 220, 229–30
Newson, Elizabeth 176
non-binary 159–60, 162
nonverbal learning disorder (NVLD) 172
normative solidarity 207–8

obligation, mutual 207–8
obsessive-compulsive disorder (OCD) 172
'olden days' 194
one-on-one time 56–8, 63, 119, 219, 225–6
oral history 193, 195
orca studies 51
outdoor games 81

Pakistan
  grandmaternal involvement 15
parental alienation 133–5, 138
  mild 133
  moderate 133
  severe 133
parental alienation syndrome 133
parenting orders 58–9
Parenting Today in Victoria 118
parents
  birth of child *see* birth of grandchild/ren
  boundaries, respecting 65
  communication with *see* communication
  conflict with child *see* conflict
  consent to posting online 55
  divorce *see* separation and divorce
  expectant, reassurance of 26–8, 219
  gifts incompatible with values 61
  grandparents, support from xix, 17
  isolation post-birth 40–1
  neutrality as to childraising 219, 229–230
  reassurance and encouragement 219, 223–4
  seeking support 46
  sleep deprivation 45–6
  unsolicited advice 219, 222–3
Parker, Gordon xviii, 187–8
pathological demand avoidance (PDA) 176, 178
'peekaboo' 80
peer pressure 52, 127, 231
personality
  determinants 71–3
  traits 53
photos 192–3
places, revisiting 192, 235
play 34 *see also* games
  attitude 86
  babies 79–80
  benefits 70, 77, 78, 83–4, 86, 226

Index

child-led 83
designated period 96
fun facts 77
innate drive 78
older children 82–4
sensory 180
structured 84
threat 86
toddlers and young children 80–2
Playgroup Australia 256
postpartum bleeding 42
postpartum depression (PPD) 42
pregnancy
honour parents' wishes 23–4, 221
questions to avoid 22–3
reaction to news 21–2, 219, 220–1
reassurer role 26–8, 219
'war stories' 26
prenatal stress 2
primary carer xii, 11, 58–9
financial support 12
reasons 12
statistics 11, 58
puberty
fear 165
'precocious puberty' 115–16

queer/questioning 146

Raising Children Network 257
Autism Hub 267–8
ReachOut 263, 265
ReachOut Schools 265–6
reading
book choices 18–19
grandchild, with 18–19, 53, 82
records
grandchild 197–8
milestones 55
oral history 195
resilience 70
building 56, 84
determinants 1, 3
main components 5–6
respect, mutual 110, 112, 118
role-play 82
router plug-ins 103
Rudd, Kevin xviii, 33–4

safety 229
online 105
physical 68
Samoa
fa'afafine 162
schizophrenia 172
screentime
alternatives 103
communication 103
designated period 96
determinants 94–8
excessive 78, 90–1, 95–6, 101
gaming *see* video gaming
internet addiction 98–100
limits 90, 102
meaning 89–90
moderation 92–3, 95
monitoring 90, 96
optimal amount 93–4

Index

parental controls 103–4
rules 97, 226
streaming services 98, 99
teaching safe use 108–9
technological solutions 103
self-minimising behaviour 53
sensory bins 180
sensory play 180
sensory processing disorder (SPD) 172
sensory sensitivities 174, 181
sensory toys 80
separation and divorce 130–1, 231–2
alienation *see* alienation
Covid-19 pandemic 132
estrangement and *see* estrangement
legal considerations 58–9, 136–7
loss and grief 135–6, 139
neutrality 142–3
parental alienation 133–5
predictors of outcome 137–8
protective factor 138
stress 137
sermonising 57
sexual orientation 153, 160
'sharenting' 104, 105
Silverstein, Merril 202–206
singing 80
sleep deprivation 45–6
Smith, Ruth 1, 3, 4
The Smith Family 264
'snail mail' 63
social media *see also* internet
'compare and despair' phenomenon 115
social skills 3
sports 83
State Library of Queensland 258
stereotypes 6–7
streaming services 98
structural solidarity 203
Student Edge 263
stupid baby names (SBNs) 39
support, practical or instrumental 207
support group 140
synaesthesia 172

Tanzania
'grandmother effect' 14, 16–17
teaching role 50, 108–9
technology
communication 34, 62–3
DVD or Blu-ray 98
moderation 95, 219
out of touch myth 8–9
parental controls 103–4
safety 105–6
screen use *see* screentime
social media *see* social media
teenagers *see* adolescence
Thailand
kathoey 162
Tourette syndrome 172
'Traditional Grandparents' 10, 218
transgender grandchild/ren 146, 156–7
acceptance and support 167–8
challenges 163
'deadnaming' 169

Index

definitions 159–60
discrimination 164, 170, 233
expression of identity 165–7
fear of puberty 165
gender-affirming care 169, 170, 233
gender dysphoria 163
medical interventions 169
mental health 164, 233
misconception 162
names and pronouns 168, 233
negative school experiences 164
population 158
role of grandparents 167–8, 170
suggested responses 168–9
suicidality 164
third gender, recognition of 158
transitioning, 169
US case example 156–7
travelling
adolescents, with 119, 126
trust 110, 112
tummy time 79
Tweedale, Eric xviii, 199–200

ultimatums 124
United States of America (US)
gender transition, case example 156–7
Native American two-spirit people 161
urinary problems, postpartum 42

values and beliefs, shared 205–6, 207
verbal fluency 53
video gaming 8–9, 61, 83, 89, 91–2
see also screentime
visitation rights 136

Warner, Jennifer 132
Warshak, Dr Richard A. 134
welfare concerns 68–9
wellness 5
Werner, Emmy 1, 2, 3, 4
'whakapapa' xix
Williamson, David xviii, 47–9
wisdom 56, 129, 216
Wyse, Lois 235

Youth Central 263
YouTube 97
YouTube Kids 97

Also by Michael Carr-Gregg

Adolescence: A guide for parents (with Erin Shale)

Surviving Year 12: A sanity kit for students and parents

Surviving Adolescents: The must-have manual for all parents

The Princess Bitchface Syndrome: Surviving adolescent girls

Real Wired Child: What parents need to know about kids online

When to Really Worry: Mental health problems in teenagers and what to do about them

Surviving Step-Families

Beyond Cyberbullying: An essential guide for parenting in the digital age

Strictly Parenting: Everything you need to know about raising school-aged kids

The Princess Bitchface Syndrome 2.0: Surviving adolescent girls (with Elly Robinson)

The Prince Boofhead Syndrome: Surviving adolescent boys (with Elly Robinson)

Surviving Adolescents 2.0: The must-have manual for parents (with Elly Robinson)

Smart Snacks (with Flip Shelton)

Surviving Year 12: An essential resource for families (with Elly Robinson)

Starting Secondary School: The essential handbook for every Australian family (with Sharon Witt)